SCIENCE AND SOCIETY

SCIENCE AND SOCIETY

The John C. Polanyi
Nobel Laureates Lectures

John Polanyi (signature)

Edited and with an Introduction by

Martin Moskovits

Martin Moskovits (signature)

Anansi

Published in 1995 by
House of Anansi Press Limited
1800 Steeles Avenue West
Concord, Ontario L4K 2P3
Tel. (416) 445-3333
Fax (416) 445-5967

Canadian Cataloguing in Publication Data

Main entry under title:
Science and society : the John C. Polanyi Nobel laureates lectures

ISBN 0-88784-170-8

1. Science. 2. Science - Social aspects.
I. Moskovits, Martin, 1943-

Q171.S3 1995   500   C95-931677-9

Cover Design: Bill Douglas / The Bang
Typography by Kinetics Design & Illustration

Group photograph on page ii by Stephen Frost
Standing, from left: Max Perutz, Michael Smith, Dudley Herschbach,
Bertram Brockhouse, John Polanyi, Christian de Duve, Charles Townes,
Henry Kendall; seated: Gerhard Hertzberg, George Porter,
James Watson, Ilya Prigogine

All photographs in main text by Jewel Randolph

Printed and bound in Canada

House of Anansi Press gratefully acknowledges the support of the
Canada Council, the Ontario Ministry of Citizenship, Culture,
and Recreation, Ontario Arts Council, and Ontario Publishing Centre
in the development of writing and publishing in Canada.

CONTENTS

Preface   *vii*

Introduction   *xi*

PART I
A LABORATORY OF ONE'S OWN

John Charles Polanyi   3
  Understanding Discovery

Dudley Robert Herschbach   11
  The Shape of Molecular Collisions

Charles Hard Townes   29
  Unpredictability in Science and Technology

PART II
LIFE: THE COSMIC IMPERATIVE

Max Perutz   45
  Living Molecules

James Dewey Watson   57
  The Human Genome Project

Michael Smith   69
    Synthetic DNA and Biology

Christian René de Duve   83
    Life as a Cosmic Imperative

PART III
    THE NEXT HALF-CENTURY

Henry Way Kendall   95
    Global Prospects

Ilya Prigogine   107
    Time, Chaos, and the Two Cultures

George Porter   123
    Chemistry Under the Sun

PREFACE

$\mathcal{A}$n unusual event took place in Toronto on November 3 and 4, 1994. Eleven Nobel laureates gathered to honour fellow laureate John Polanyi, who had recently taken up the John Polanyi Chair in Chemistry, established by the Jackman Foundation. So large an assembly of Nobel laureates was unprecedented, at least outside Stockholm. Its uniqueness was celebrated through a host of activities, the centrepiece being a series of public lectures on the theme Science and Society. The laureates' visit caught the interest of the media across Canada. One journalist described the atmosphere as "electric."

The first day began with a well-attended press conference held in the Council Chambers of the University of Toronto and hosted by Canadian broadcaster Adrienne Clarkson. One question stands out, underscoring to some extent the cynicism that currently exists about the benefits of science and the motives of scientists, in Canada and elsewhere. A reporter asked if the celebration was primarily to solicit more money for research. Present in that room, among others, were the discoverers of the structures of DNA and hemoglobin; the discoverer of the lysosomes; the inventor of the maser, on which the laser was based; and one of the premier elucidators of the structure of the nucleus.

The laureates were bussed to the Ontario Legislative Building after the press conference, where they were luncheon guests of the lieutenant governor of Ontario, the Honourable Henry Jackman. Later, they were welcomed to the Legislature by members of the provincial parliament. A strange occurrence took place after the laureates left the Legislature. Seven of them were trapped in an elevator descending from the Speaker's gallery to the main floor. While several people searched frantically for the missing laureates, those confined passed the time away singing Gilbert and Sullivan songs. This incident was reported widely in the media, and even made a society column.

In the meantime, people were already pressing to get seated in Convocation Hall to await the arrival of the laureates. The hall seats approximately 1,700. The lectures were to have begun at 2:30 P.M. and, well before that hour, almost 3,000 people arrived, some from as far away as New York state and other provinces. We had foreseen that the lectures might overfill Convocation Hall, and had arranged for a microwave link to a full-size video projector in Hart House Theatre to accommodate the overflow audience. This 450-seat theatre did not suffice for the 800 or so who arrived there, having been denied entrance to Convocation Hall. The video technician at Hart House became alarmed at the mood of the crowd, and hurriedly set up a large speaker outside the theatre. The twenty-minute delay from the elevator incident, coming at the end of an hour or more of frenzied seat-claiming, raised the expectant mood of the audience to such a pitch that when the twelve Nobel laureates finally filed onto the stage, the audience rose and broke into a tumultuous ovation.

All in all, the tenor of the event was summarized best by Dudley Herschbach, who was overheard saying, "What we have here is the Woodstock of science."

The Polanyi inauguration event could not have been possible without the efforts of Bluma Appel, Adrienne Clarkson, the Hon. Barnett Danson, Darlene Frampton, Cynthia Goh, the Hon. Alastair Gillespie, Kim Luke, Nona Macdonald Heaslip, Derrick Heyd, William Kilbourn, Sue McClelland, Sue Polanyi, Mary Alice Stuart, Gary E. Turner, Helen Vari, and Stephen Wallace.

There is an enormous difference between public lectures and a published book. In making the transformation from recorded transcripts to printed essays, all the original "texts" have experienced change, to a greater or a lesser degree. As editor of the book, I have incurred many debts: to Bruce Westwood, whose idea it was; to Alida Minchella, who has a gift for the written word, and to Rosemary Shipton, who fine-tuned the text.

Martin Moskovits

INTRODUCTION

"*H*as science been good for society?" Although this question is never posed explicitly, the struggle to answer it informs the entire lecture series. Ultimately, a hopeful consensus develops. The answer may seem obvious when asked of ten individuals whose entire lives have revolved around science, but this remarkable group of individuals possess a subtlety of argument and acuity of observation which induces their vision to transcend the obvious. It is the question itself that is booby-trapped. The meaning of the word *society,* as it is understood today, is so suffused with the results and symbols of science to make the answer a tautology. Still, there remains the nagging feeling that, like the magic of the sorcerer's apprentice, the benefits of science are commingled with a certain lack of control.

Ilya Prigogine expresses the dualism of science most directly. Science has layered its advances with a potential for destruction, but he regards this good-with-evil character as an attribute of civilization, and not specifically of science. Henry Kendall sounds the most foreboding warning regarding science's potential for harm. His concern revolves around the question of overpopulation. The phenomenal growth of the human race is due almost entirely to the eradication of disease and the development of modern agricultural technologies. However, he, along with the other contributors, is genuinely convinced that science and technology can provide the tools for addressing these serious problems.

Is there a means of channelling scientific research so that it produces only what is good and useful? In other words, "can we find a way to do science which has, from the outset, only the potential for good?" Today's most debated policy question relates to the possibility of directing scientific research towards predictably *useful* — as in economically rewarding — targets. Is it possible to restrict the generation of knowledge to areas that will produce new business while avoiding those areas of knowledge that will not? Most scientists do not believe it is possible. Aside from the fact that it requires a prophetic ability about the direction in which both business and science are heading, the assumption that research can be strategically directed assumes an understanding of the mysteries and mechanisms of innovation. Nevertheless, there are many economists, politicians, and civil servants who think so. Charles Townes delivers a compelling argument against this notion, maintaining that innovation in scientific research is a complex phenomenon which depends on so many variables that its behaviour is more readily described by complexity theory. The directions that lead to useful or desirable innovations are inherently unpredictable, much like the precise date or the severity of storms. Continuing the storm metaphor, he points out that we can be fairly confident that in any given year there will be a certain number of storms within a certain range of severity, but we cannot predict where or when they'll hit. So with scientific innovation. We can be sure that major discoveries will continue to be made; we just can't tell where and when success will be achieved. The many examples he cites of the major discoveries missed by individuals asked to prophesy the development of science illustrate the point. In this regard, scientists fare no better than others. They, however, have learned the futility of trying to second-guess science's chaotic pattern of success. Instead, they, along with Townes, recommend that the most prudent policy is to ensure that research be broad-based and that we place our bets on talented people rather than on strategic research planning.

The conclusion that the usefulness of research is hard to direct through research strategies also suggests that the harmful effects of science are, likewise, difficult to control through research policies. That control must come from growth in wisdom in other domains such as governance and politics. Scientists know this fact perhaps better than most thinkers. It is for this reason that so many of them, like John Polanyi and Henry Kendall, spend a large portion of their lives organizing, educating, and arguing for reason in arms control and environmental policies. Further removing the direction of science from the hands of scientists would actually delay the process of refining the use of science for good. The same lack of wisdom that had allowed the fruits of science to be marshalled towards poor ends would be active in a policy that attempts to solve problems through a form of scientific censorship.

No story better illustrates the rapidity of the development of a field than the story of modern molecular genetics. In just thirty years, we progressed from the fundamental knowledge of the structure of DNA to the human genome project, which will map out the millions of human genes. The field has matured so rapidly that one of its major areas of debate and scholarship currently is not technical, but moral, ethical, and philosophical. James Watson takes us lucidly from the early days of molecular genetics through to the ethical questions that are emerging with the imminent knowledge of our physical destiny and that of our children. We will know which diseases we have inherited and which we will pass on to our progeny. Ultimately, as we learn more about the link (if any) between groups of genes and subtle attributes such as intelligence, physical strength, and body type, we will be able to predict many of the traits that we are likely to bestow on our children, or that we have already bestowed on an unborn child. What choices can we rightly make when we possess such knowledge? Should we tailor-make our children to so great an extent that even the eye colour is selected?

Max Perutz describes vividly the difficulty with which the genetic role of DNA was discovered by Oswald Avery. Up until then, genes were thought to be carried by proteins. No one was willing to believe that so boring a molecule as DNA, made up as it is from sugar, phosphate, and four simple organic bases, was the selfish emissary chosen to carry so important a message.

Michael Smith illustrates how, once the truth about DNA was known, techniques for manipulating genes, cleaving DNA into millions of bits and then recombining them with the genetic material of a bacterium, became routine. Ultimately, it resulted in one of the major technological advances of the twentieth century — biotechnology.

Knowledge of the structure of the genetic code also resulted in one of the major puzzles regarding the origin of life and the likelihood that life can arise again, or that life (such as the life on Earth) can arise elsewhere. DNA encodes the synthesis of proteins. An organism's entire physical structure is written in its DNA. The code is written in "words" containing four letters. If a strand of DNA contains one million of these letters, then there are $4^{1,000,000}$ or approximately $10^{600,000}$ different possible DNA strands of that length. A DNA strand one million letters long is, in fact, a rather short example. Human DNA is many times longer than that. Nevertheless, the number of possibilities is unimaginably great — so great that the probability that any one of them could have occurred by chance in the five or so billion years that Earth has existed is infinitesimally small. When one asks a biologist to estimate how many of the possible configurations would result in a viable organism, the answer would be "very few, almost none," implying either that the particular strands of DNA harboured by life on Earth did not happen by accident or that life is an incredible accident never to be repeated again.

Christian de Duve argues against such a pessimistic view. He contends that life proceeds through a series of very probable events — incredibly probable ones. Since the number of steps leading to the evolution of an organism is huge, and since the final probability of its existence is the product of the probabilities that each of the steps is completed successfully, only steps that are extremely probable can lead to an even moderately probable organism. In other words, the appearance of life must have been an imperative. If so, life will exist wherever conditions are conducive for its existence throughout the universe.

It is said that science concerns itself with structure, while purpose is the domain of philosophy or religion. The discoveries of the twentieth century, quantum mechanics and molecular biology, have blurred the traditional solitudes of structure and purpose. Structure is still a powerful paradigm in science, but the apparent collapse of strict determinism that accompanied the development of quantum mechanics has inspired some scientists to cross the philosophical line. They dare ask questions about the possible link between the apparent indeterminism of the outcome of quantum mechanical experiments and the freedom of the human spirit. Ilya Prigogine argues that science (even the classical science of Newton and Maxwell) need not be seen as the realm of determinism. Rather, both classical and modern science can be recast in terms of probabilities. Deterministic science sees the universe as an automaton which, set into motion, has a perfectly predictable future, provided that the calculation can be carried out to a sufficient level of precision. One need no longer construct a science based on mathematics which predicts a precise (but ultimately wrong) future outcome; a new science can be constructed whose mathematical description deals with probabilities *a priori*. The outcome of any given set of circumstances would be in doubt, but the distribution of outcomes would be a robust feature of this new science. In Prigogine's opinion, this new science would not only describe more accurately the way the universe really behaves, but it would also be more consonant with the way human beings perceive such variables as time. The underlying chaos that is a pervasive feature of nature — chaos that makes two closely similar sets of circumstances unfold in such a way that in the long run their futures have little in common — this chaos rests upon the fact that systems are non-linear. In a non-linear system, the magnitude of an effect is not proportional to the size of the cause; instead, the result grows more rapidly or more slowly than merely proportional. It is also often the case that a little of the result will feed back, adding to the cause. This feedback can lead to chaos, much like the way a microphone in front of the speaker broadcasting its sound can lead to an ear piercing screech, shattering the sound into unrecognizable chaotic noise.

Prigogine finds great solace in a universe in which the basic laws of science are not deterministic but rather probabilistic. He notes that in the development of civilization, with its underpinning of technology, laws of science and determinism have brought both benefits and ills to humanity. The most serious evil of civilization is the establishment of castes, in which the privileges and powers of the upper caste, the rulers, are much greater than those of the lower. This, in his words, is a form and a cause of violence. Wars are waged at the expense of members of the lower castes for the benefit of the privileged. This unfortunate evolution is illustrated by the development of tombs and burial ceremonies along with the emergence of civilization. The near-uniformity of neolithic tombs suggests that, in those cultures, the tombs of chiefs and the common people did not differ appreciably, implying, in turn, that all neolithic people shared an almost equal social status. Contrast this situation with the Egyptian, Chinese, or Mesoamerican civilizations, where the tombs of the pharaohs were giant pyramids, those of court scribes were elaborate tombs, while the common Egyptians were interred in simple pits. The same is true of the Chinese nobility and the Mayan upper classes. All these cultures also evolved highly complex calendars and systems for astronomical observations, perhaps the most deterministic of sciences. This might imply that the fundamental violence characterizing civilization comes about from the inevitability of privilege that flows out of a deterministic world view. An even more subtle interpretation of Prigogine's position is that the deterministic character of science developed in response to the innately fatalistic nature of culture. With the development of non-deterministic science we are poised, for the first time in history, for a radical redirection of the basic forces that have driven humankind towards the development of culture. Once a new physics is established based on probability rather than certainty, the violent side of civilization may be tempered along with the cockiness that is engendered by our attachment to determinism, thereby improving the balance between the good and the evil endowments of civilization. In so doing one might also restore society's optimistic view of science.

Amazingly, mathematicians have shown that the same non-linearities that lead to chaos can produce orderly patterns: the stripes of the zebra, the periodic ripples in the sand on the beach, and the whorls in smoke rising from a snuffed-out candle. Indeed, it was science's curiosity about these orderly shapes that has led it to its current enlightenment about chaos. Shape, and especially beautiful shape, has been a powerful motivating force in science. Discovering that the DNA molecule had the simple and symmetrical architecture of a double helix — two spiral staircases rising to the same floors, one leading the other as in the château at Chambord — undoubtedly enhanced the rapidity with which molecular biology advanced. Things just wouldn't have been the same had the genetic principle been consigned to a shapeless complex mass without order and symmetry.

But molecular shape is not the only shape that excites chemists. By making two molecules that are about to react (thereby making a new product) travel along straight lines by confining each to its own "molecular beam" and allowing them to intersect at only one spot, one can look for patterns in the direction in which the products fan out. Amazingly, this pattern is seldom random and chaotic. Often the reaction products fly off in very specific directions from the point of intersection of the two beams. Dudley Herschbach describes how the shape of these trajectories can reveal the most intimate details about how molecules react. He points out that the technique of studying reactions in molecular beams is restricted to special cases. Surprisingly, he finds that what he and others had learned about chemical reaction in this way had enormous generality. His work and that of John Polanyi and Yuan Lee resulted in global paradigms about chemical reactions which underlie all our knowledge of chemical reactivity, including the reactivity of the largest and most complex systems. He also points out that the development of this mature branch of science resulted from "crazy" experiments dismissed at the outset to be unworkable.

Innovations in science and advances in knowledge often have unforeseen repercussions in areas of concern far from the original intent of the research. This point is illustrated in Lord Porter's lecture. He asks another global question: "Can the human race survive?" Henry Kendall also asks this question, but in the context of numbers; Lord Porter poses his in terms of energy. His conclusion is simple. Oil and gas will run out in two or three generations. Unless we can develop technologies such as nuclear fusion, solar energy is our best hope as a sustained energy source. Nuclear fusion, the other possible long-term solution, has not been accomplished economically as yet, and forecasts for its development are unreliable. (Lord Porter does not remark on the role of nuclear fission.) He sees solar energy not only as a source of electricity or heat, but also as a harvestable crop. He sees a future in which fuel-bearing plants are grown and harvested entirely as a source of transportable fuel, much as petroleum is today. The difference is that it would be renewable.

How does all this link to the statement that advances in scientific knowledge can have an impact on issues far from the original intent? Lord Porter's major tool, one which harks back to the subject of his Nobel award, is ultrafast dynamical studies: an investigation of rates at which chemical reactions and, in particular, reactions initiated by light, take place. Great scientists like Lord Porter are attracted to the fundamental and complex photochemical reactions that accompany chemical processes, such as vision and photosynthesis. Photosynthesis is a chain of chemical processes in which eight photons of light are absorbed in light–harvesting organelles containing chlorophyll. The photons cause electrons to be transferred between chemical species, eventually causing water and carbon dioxide to be converted into oxygen and carbohydrates. The series of steps in this process includes, among many, a rapid transfer of energy between two chlorophyll pools and an ensuing electron transfer. All these steps occur very fast, on time scales that must be measured in picoseconds or less. A picosecond is 1 million-millionth of a second. A major point here is that the rate of food or fuel production by a green plant is limited by the slowest step in the numerous steps involved in photosynthesis. If this step were hastened, the efficiency with which sunlight is converted to usable fuel would be increased. One step (although not the slowest) was determined to take twenty-one picoseconds in the photosynthetic apparatus possessed by green plants. Interestingly, it was found to take only three picoseconds in the light-gathering pigments of purple bacteria. Biochemists have determined that the proteins making up those two systems differ very little — they differ in the identity of only a single amino acid. (This also illustrates the relative shortness of time associated with heredity as seen through the eyes of their fundamental chemistry. Despite the vast external difference between green plants and purple bacteria, their genetic kinship is written in their DNA, which eventually is expressed in the proteins they fabricate.)

Present-day techniques of genetic engineering are, in principle, able to modify the structure of the proteins involved in photo-synthesis so that the rapid electron transfer characteristic of light-harvesting bacteria is incorporated into a green plant. If the same strategy is applied to the slowest step, the fuel production rate of that plant should then increase several-fold. Perhaps one can pick an oil-producing shrub and genetically engineer it to produce oil five times faster than it does now. This plant would become the fuel crop of the future.

The strategy for improving the fuel production of plants would have been difficult to develop, if not impossible, were it not for the ultrafast rate studies such as those carried out by Lord Porter and his co-workers. In turn, those studies would have been impossible were it not for the development of ultrafast lasers by physicists and physical chemists for purposes that were unlinked to studies of photosynthesis. Lasers can be made to emit pulses, flashes of laser light like the bursts of light from a camera flash. The camera flash emits bursts that last a mere one-thousandth or one ten-thousandth of a second, whereas modern lasers can produce pulses with durations shorter than ten femtoseconds. One femtosecond is one over one thousand million million seconds. Little did the developers of these fast lasers think that the world's future energy strategy might hinge on their inventions.

Lord Porter estimates that with currently available green plants, we would need to convert some 11 percent of the world's cultivatable land towards fuel production. With genetic engineered plants, that number might drop to just over 2 percent, a very workable number — if world demand for fuel does not rise drastically in the interim.

Henry Kendall warns that such demand is unavoidable if world population growth does not cease, and indeed reverse. He sees the ever growing number of human beings as today's gravest environmental issue, and also the one least actively pursued by the environmental movement. To some extent this is due to the fact that the environmental movement lacks an international perspective. To be sure, countries can get together to agree on an international ban on CFCs, as they did in producing the so-called Montreal protocol. But in Kendall's words, this was in response to an obviously felt injury; in that case the injury was the disappearance of the ozone layer over the poles, which will unquestionably result in increased cases of cancer due to the enhanced exposure to ultraviolet radiation from the sun. The environmental movement seems to have succeeded only in cases where human activities result in damage that is manifestly clear or where the potential for harm is obvious.

The rampant increase in the world's population is an even more dangerous and much more pervasive problem, which seems to be unfolding without engendering the fierce response from environmentalists that has been so successful in forcing governments to enact pollution control legislation in many Western nations. This accelerating pace of numbers is putting enormous pressure on agriculture and demand for energy. The loss of tropical forest and the reduction of arable land to desert result from the insatiable demand for agricultural land on the one hand and from poor agricultural practices on the other. In many of the most populated areas of the world, the land under cultivation is almost at its limit. Although we get glimpses of the impending global disaster in the famines and disease that result when daily life is perturbed by a natural disaster or by war, these disturbances pale in comparison with the events that will occur when the limits to population growth are finally reached (in the next fifty to one hundred years). Nature will "correct" those pressures through draconian measures that boggle the imagination. Lest we think that we in the West can be complacent, believing that this problem is one of the "other world," not ours, Kendall reminds us that the ills resulting from population pressure in the developing world have already resulted in demands for immigration that will increase as the problem grows.

Grave though it is, the problem is not hopeless. It is our responsibility in the West, and especially the responsibility of scientists who understand the issues clearly, to bring these problems to the attention of political and religious leaders. Although the solution to this problem is technological, its implementation hinges upon ethical and political moves — a chillingly discouraging prospect against which only scientists' hopeful optimism can prevail.

Has science been good for society? Certainly it has made us the premier species of the planet, at least for now. It has also elevated the human race to the state of spiritual sophistication in which it feels compelled to ask the question, and stands a chance of formulating an answer. One of science's most positive attributes is its inherent and consistent opposition to despotism. Galileo's observations have outlived papal infallibility, and Mendel's experiments have prevailed against Lysenko and Stalin. Science is also the only philosophy with a consistent record of prediction in areas where the prophecy is not obvious. While Hegel's dialectic would conclude that there could be only seven planets just days before the discovery of the eighth, and religious doctrine insisted that comets existed below the moon's orbit, science would correctly predict thousands of phenomena. So successful has science been that its accomplishments are routinely trivialized. The telephone is far more reliable than telepathy for remote communication, yet it is telepathy that is regarded by millions as a sublime mystery despite its hit-and-miss track record. The case for an affirmative answer to our fundamental question is strong, but as Chou En Lai responded when asked if the French Revolution had been a good thing, "It may be too early to tell."

Science Policy and Research Motivation

Science policy in North America is undergoing a revolution of a novel variety. This revolution has already produced great changes in the research programs of American industry and in the research strategies being formulated by American universities. Because American science has such an enormous profile internationally, this revolution is bound to be felt worldwide. Certainly, it is influencing science policy in Canada, which has always imitated U.S. policy, sometimes in an exaggerated way, and it will affect science in the emerging democracies, many of which look to America for workable models. I believe that the American system of letting peer review set the scientific agenda, of funding research on the basis of excellence as the first criterion, of ensuring that the full spectrum of activities from fundamental research to development is carried out within the country, and of encouraging industry to do its own research and development in areas pertinent to its business is a wise and successful system. It is, in fact, this system that is currently under siege. The "new" system is not new at all. Indeed, elements of it have been proposed time and again. What makes things different now is that, in the past, proponents of the new system were generally vanquished successfully. Today they are the victors. What I am talking about is the ascent of the view that discovery can be predicted, that there is a science of discovery which should allow scientists to find a shortcut from desire to implementation. Up until now, so the old guard would say, one investigated nature guided mainly by the need to understand and to discover. As discoveries added to our knowledge, they would suggest applications either to the discoverers themselves or to others who would integrate the new discoveries into their own list of wishes and goals. To ensure that an abundance of applications could be made, an even larger number of research programs had to be supported in a very broad range of research areas. One person expressed this strategy as, "If you wish to find a prince, be prepared to kiss many frogs."

Proponents of this system point to many hundreds of discoveries that eventually led to entirely new industries unconceived as goals before the discovery. The most famous, of course, are the transistor and the laser. But more modern examples, such as the fullerenes, high T_c superconductors, and scanning microscopy, are also plentiful. Likewise, the earnest application of resources to a very focused goal doesn't ensure success. More money has been spent on cancer research than on any other field, and a great deal of progress has been made, yet a general treatment for cancer has not yet been achieved.

I suppose the debate is not unlike one between Darwinists and Lamarckians. The former state that one should make discoveries broadly and that something useful will result through a process of selection. The latter say that this process is too wasteful to support and that scientists should only work towards strategic targets so that their efforts are well focused. Of course, the debate has a great deal of subtlety in it, such as the role of talent, inspiration, and the psychology of discovery. In some ways, it is these subtleties that will determine which of the two strategies is the natural one and, therefore, the one to follow.

Why are the Lamarckians prevailing? It is because a new breed of individuals are taking interest in science policy. In the United States, science policy used to be the purview of a very few politicians, primarily ones with some technical bent, who generally sought advice from scientists and engineers. Currently, scientists are viewed with increasing suspicion as irresponsible advocates of self-serving policies that allow them to "play" at discovery while important national issues are ignored. Many more politicians are taking an interest in science and scientists, and they find naive scientists easy targets for scoring points with the public. Moreover, the economists have now discovered science and technology policy, and dozens of articles on research policy appear in North America each year written by economists. If you want to know what nearly all of them conclude, you need only quote from a recent article entitled "How the Developed Countries Became Rich" by Nathan Rosenberg, a famous economist from Stanford University. Rosenberg writes, "The conclusion seems inescapable that a first-rate basic research community has, in the past, been neither a necessary nor a sufficient condition for success in the commercial exploitation of scientific knowledge."[1] Although the article is rife with technical economic detail, its gist, like that of others, is that Japan does no fundamental research, yet Japan is rich; therefore, there's no need for us to continue doing fundamental research, or at least we should restrict it sharply. Of course, the major premise is wrong; Japan does a great deal of fundamental research; it is just that until recently, it didn't do it particularly well. Nevertheless, it did and still does it, and spends lots of money doing it.

The new perspective is spreading with alarming speed. The cancellation of the superconducting supercollider after it had been begun is one manifestation. The relentless rhetoric by American politicians on the subject of what they perceive to be wasteful research, suggesting that research should all be aligned towards pre-identified industrial goals, is having a dramatic effect. Most major new sources of funding now support so-called targeted research. All this has prompted one writer to state that we are entering the age of democratic research policy. The writer was referring to the statement of Isidor Rabi, the American Nobel laureate and father of nuclear magnetic resonance, who once stated, "in physics some guy from Podunk doesn't have the same vote as Fermi." Nowadays, it seems, this is no longer true.

American industry has already accepted many of the premises of the new model. There is a pervasive attitude among CEOs of industry that they have not been getting value for the investment made in the research of the past decade. I am not speaking just of industries like the petroleum companies, where the role of research was not always well defined and research programs would expand and contract in unpredictable ways. It is in companies like AT&T Bell, IBM, and Xerox, which traditionally made money through innovation, that this trend is most alarming. IBM cut its research effort by more than half. Companies like Xerox, Kodak, and Du Pont quickly followed, or in some cases preceded IBM in this move. Some, unlike IBM, were not under excessive financial stress. At AT&T the cuts were not as dramatic, but the change in philosophy was just as stark.

What is most evident is that the motive is not financial but ideological. The fraction of the entire U.S. research and development budget that goes to fundamental research is very small. It is an even smaller fraction of the overall R&D budgets of the industrial laboratories mentioned above. To go after this small fraction with such vehemence means that saving money is not the main issue; rather, it is the belief that the new scheme will create more wealth than the old.

This newly discovered paradigm for creating inventions is really a rediscovery. Alchemy was an early form of targeted research. The alchemist was instructed to have a single mission: convert a base metal into gold. Along the way, the science of chemistry was created. Some disappointed funding agencies, in those days kings, princes, and nobles, undoubtedly cut off more than the alchemist's grant when he or she discovered phosphoric acid instead of producing gold.

If we are going towards a new model for making valuable discoveries, it is important for us to consider what the chances of success are through the new model. An important question to ask is what motivates people to make discoveries and how the ordinary citizen who pays the bill perceives this process.

Views of science cover a broad scale of perception, ranging

from the deeply hostile to the utopian. Certainly the most common anti-science view results from the notion that science has created weapons of destruction and terror which the world would have been better off without. In the movie *Straw Dogs*, the local priest, when introduced to the protagonist, a mathematician, asks him immediately, "Can you deny your guilt for the atomic bomb?" Although the response was victorious, religion being so nakedly exposed as a source of human misery, nevertheless, the point was clear: every scientist is personally guilty for the creation of the bomb. It is the science equivalent of Original Sin. A more recent version of this view is one voiced by environmentalists who point to science and scientists as authors of global rape and destruction. Theirs is a familiar case.

Impersonal coldness is a familiar image of science and scientists in art and literature. Science is regarded as orthogonal to the human side of the human being. An example is the cruel scientist, Anthime, in André Gide's novel *L'Aventure de Lafcadio*. Others see scientists as impious iconoclasts who have removed absolutes from human life, and science as a usurping culture replacing Christianity as the main source of new symbols. Neo-orthodox theologians call science the "self-estrangement" of humankind because it leads them into realms where no ultimate, that is, religious, concerns prevail. Even more conservative theologians believe that the quest for knowledge of the external world is a legacy of Original Sin, in which the scientist seeks to know what is forbidden; it is impious, they say, for humankind to seek to change, through technology, the world that God granted us.

Science has also been attacked as being un- or even anti-intellectual. José Ortega writes in his book *The Revolt of the Masses* that science is an intellectually bankrupt pursuit which automatically converts the scientist into "mass-man, makes of him a primitive, a modern barbarian. Experimental science has progressed thanks in great part to the work of men astoundingly mediocre, and even less than mediocre. That is to say, modern science...finds a place for the intellectually commonplace man and allows him to work therein with success."[2] Kenneth Boulding sees science "as the process of substituting unimportant questions which *can* be answered for important ones which *cannot*."[3] The conclusion drawn from these views is that the scientist is at worst a being without social or moral conscience, and at best an intellectual lightweight who performs often trivial or useless experiments with little intellectual content.

Not all views of science are negative. Some hold fast to the optimistic visions born at the turn of the twentieth century and reaching its zenith in the 1950s, in which science and technology could solve all problems — mechanical, medical, and agricultural — with no negative side-effects. On the contrary, the prospect of a well-fed, healthy, literate, and prosperous humanity suggested that wars would end, suffering and drudgery would be abated, and, as a result, the more superstitious aspects of religion and the more dangerous elements of philosophy, such as nationalism, would disappear, to be replaced by a "more scientific" view of the world. Others take science as the template in which to formulate non-scientific — literary, social, and moral — conclusions. Our language is full of words and symbols alluding to science. We speak of equilibrium, feedback, input, conservation of energy, invariance, and quantum jump. We extrapolate relativity to matters of religion and ethics, speaking of relative truths and different viewpoints due to different frames of reference.

All extreme views of science are dangerous. Moreover, science as an intellectual and cultural activity should be distinguished from its application through technology. The former is uncontrollable, since it is ultimately about ideas. The latter could and should be subject to social policy and economic constraints. The confusion between science as an intellectual activity and technology is alarmingly general. Yet there is no such confusion regarding the distinction between psychology and advertising, economics and fiscal policy, political science and politics, or religious philosophy and church doctrines. Despite the fact that the implementation of economic and political theories has almost certainly resulted in the death and suffering of millions, political science and economics are not generally held to account, and the potential danger contained in those two disciplines is not generally feared. By contrast, science is held responsible for the negative aspects of technology. Medicine, however, is still regarded very positively, even though one could claim that the explosive growth of the world's population and its environmental consequences is largely due to the eradication of disease by modern medical science.

The scientific method is also sometimes seen to work in reverse — that theory precedes experiment and that science is a vast ego trip in which scientists attempt to gather only facts which support a preconceived notion. This attitude was illustrated by some of the news reporting surrounding "cold fusion." Some reporters saw the scepticism of many scientists to the report that cold fusion had been achieved as attempts to squelch this important discovery in order to protect their turf.

The scientific method cannot be inverted, because it is not the sole domain of the scientist. The scientific method is not an invention. It has been used by all people since creation. It is the method of applied observation which is used instinctively every day to make judgments about what will work and what will not. The ancient academic community abhorred intellectual pursuits involving experimentation. When this tradition was reversed during the Renaissance, it appeared that a sublime and mysterious discovery had been made. Nothing could be less mysterious. The empirical method is based on inductive reasoning, that undefined mental process whereby a person proceeds from the particular to the general. This process appears to be an innate human function observed even in infants, who have had little time to be corrupted.

Much of the fear of the scientific method stems from ignorance. Most people feel that the scientific method involves little or no faith or any human aspect, that everything must be proved in dry, epicene ways. How else would rational thought and human good be construed to be antithetical?

Briefly, the first step in the empirical method entails observing the world, whether through a contrived experiment, just looking around, or through introspection. To say that curiosity motivates science is to say that the process ends there, and certainly it does end there with most people.

Scientists go further, however, driven by a zeal to systematize and condense. They make models which express the underlying pattern in the observations, then quantify these models by applying the postulates of a system, such as Newton's laws or the postulates of quantum mechanics. The concept of a system — a set of postulates plus a mechanism for applying them — was known to the Greeks. They, however, had no concept of the *rejection* of postulates which characterizes the scientific method, but rather assumed the postulates to be absolute truths. Herein lies one of the conceptual problems. If science looks for truth, how can one have constantly shifting postulates? The obvious answer is that science is motivated by the search for truth in an asymptotic sense. Consequently, if one needs absolute truth immediately, one must look elsewhere, perhaps in a religion or a philosophy. It should be pointed out in passing that philosophy has defied systematization, as is evident from *The Ethics* of Spinoza, which is written in a postulatory form and yet arrives at preconceived conclusions. Whether it is meaningful to look for absolute truths is another question too broad for this, and perhaps any, discussion.

If scientists know that absolute truth will be elusive, what, then, motivates their immediate search? I believe that the impetus to condense data into theory originates from an aesthetic sense, the same sense that inspires artists — the need to find and express the simplifying principles contained in the observation of the world around us. We consider a theory elegant and great when it is able to integrate and simplify as many phenomena in as simple and conservative a fashion as possible. The same criteria are applied to great art. For example, it is generally conceded that Goya and Turner improved their art as their style evolved from a complex to a more simple and austere one.

How similar this was to the work of James Clerk Maxwell, who was able to unify all classical, electrostatic, electrodynamic, magnetostatic, magnetodynamic, electromagnetic, and optical effects into one phenomenon describable by four rather simple equations. In fact, it was this drive to unify which directed

Maxwell to the conclusion that light has electromagnetic origins. Three of the four Maxwell equations are direct restatements of expressions known before the time of Maxwell: Coulomb's law, Faraday's law, and the absence of free magnetic poles. When he combined these laws with Ampere's law from magnetostatics, Maxwell realized that this equation was inconsistent with the rest since it violated the continuity of charge and current, and, therefore, it had to be modified. This was the crucial insight that gave birth to the concept of electromagnetic waves.

The physical laws which constitute our theories, and which simplify our perception of nature, are purely human constructs. Nature does not conform to them — nature being infinitely more complex than our theories in the same way that the subject portrayed in a painting is more complex than the painting itself. Consider the famous and powerful prehistoric cave painting of a horse discovered in the Lascaux cave. It is obvious at a glance that part of the power of the painting stems from the fact that not all the details of the horse are given — some are implied — and we are grateful for and moved by that simplification. This, then, is art's great appeal, and science's, too, except that this aspect of science is not as generally known as is art's; that both provide simplified versions of our environment to hide behind when things get too complicated. Science, like art, is very much a thing of the spirit. And while it is fashionable for some scientists to consider the philosophical implications of their discoveries — for instance, what quantum theory has done to concepts of causality — it is not the philosophical but the aesthetic motives that drive most scientists.

It is an abuse of science and the scientific method when they are applied in non-scientific territory. The theory of relativity, in fact, modified the laws of mechanics and electrodynamics so that phenomena which are seen to be different by observers as a result of their relative motion can be reconciled; and no stretch of the imagination can make the theory of relativity applicable to inter-personal transactions. It certainly does not justify a blanket statement that all things are relative.

In social matters, too, pseudo-scientific methods are applied, thereby often obscuring the real issues. *Business Week*, for example, once reported the results of a study about store robberies in the United States as follows: "Then WBSI chose 60 stores for testing and 60 equally attractive stores to serve as a control group. It instituted the experimental changes at the 60 test stores, left the others alone, and monitored the results from January to August, 1975. By August, the control stores had experienced 57 armed robberies while the test group had had 40 — 30% less." The article gives the impression that by applying a scientific approach, a great benefit was achieved — 30 percent reduction in crime. This inference obfuscates the real issue — that it is unacceptable, indeed, terrifying to have sixty stores robbed forty times in eight months — and that the real question lies in a domain outside science.

Aside from providing gains in comfort and material goods, of which Western nations have enough already, science is an intellectual enterprise of great cultural importance and beauty. Science is *not* antithetical to spiritual things, but can be counted among them. The moment science is no longer seen solely in terms of its possible technological advances, many justifiable arguments against science are destroyed.

The notion should also be dispelled that scientists do what they do to save humankind. The recognition that this statement is false has fomented some of the resentment towards science, alienating the scientist from the average person. How can one feel close to an individual who professes an altruism that common people never expect from themselves?

What have these arguments to say about the proper model for the "Science of Discovery?" The notion that an aesthetic sense drives discovery is not new, as French mathematician Jacques Hadamard outlines in his fascinating book *The Psychology of Invention in the Mathematical Field*. In considering the question of insight and inspiration, and particularly the instantaneous flash of original insight that often characterizes important discoveries, he cites Henri Poincaré's discovery of the so-called Fuchsian functions. After puzzling consciously over the problem for a long time, Poincaré states:

> I left Caen, where I was living, to go on a geologic excursion under the auspices of the School of Mines. The incidents of the travel made me forget my mathematical work. Having reached Contance, we entered an omnibus to go to some place or other. At the moment when I put my foot on the step, the idea came to me, without anything in my former thought seeming to have paved the way for it, that the transformations I had used to define the Fuchsian functions were identical with those of non-Euclidean geometry. I did not verify the idea; I should not have had time, as upon taking my seat on the omnibus, I went on with a conversation already commenced, but I felt perfect certainty. On my return to Caen, for convenience sake, I verified the result at my leisure.[4]

Very complicated new ideas often occur to scientists in a flash of inspiration, frequently accompanied, as in Poincaré's case, with a heady feeling of certainty that defies logic. Yet the feeling is often right, as if there is a kind of mental shortcut that operates at such times which replaces the laborious process of deductive proof. British mathematician Roger Penrose, in his popular book *The Emperor's New Mind*, suggests that only a non-algorithmic theory of consciousness can explain this human faculty, also known as insight or inspiration or intuition.[5]

It is clear that the certitude which accompanies inspiration is connected with an aesthetic sense. We feel sure that the idea is correct without testing it because we see it as a single irreducible and beautiful whole, just as we sense a work of art to be beautiful at a single glance without subjecting it to reductionist measurements or arguments. Some of the most important scientific theories seem to have been discovered in flashes of insight induced by meagre experimental evidence (for example, general relativity). One might easily believe that this sort of inspirational process operates with *all* successful scientists whose daily concerns and accomplishments are perhaps more modest than those of a Newton, an Einstein, or a Feynman.

If so, then most fundamental solutions to problems are not made through a deductive process but through induction, which is closely linked to intuition. Intuition is an imprecisely defined concept, yet its operation is too widely experienced for its existence as a genuine process to be doubted. Most people can be trained to improve their inductive capability, but not everyone excels. There are geniuses of induction or intuition just as there are musical geniuses. Of course, intuition is not flawless. That is why it is necessary to subject flashes of insight and the feelings of aesthetic delight which accompany them to rigorous proof based on deductive reasoning. Yet it is induction that seems to initiate the truly innovative solutions to problems.

Deduction is totally algorithmic, but induction requires an undefined faculty for it to operate effectively. A computer can be programmed to deduce correct conclusions from premises, but it will not be able to intuit a correct and original generalization from a few and apparently unconnected particulars. This is characteristic of the living mind. Target-oriented research, beloved of those who administer science, will eventually fail. It is based on the assumption that solutions flow from the application of deductive reasoning to clearly defined premises.

Deduction is an important process for constructing proofs, systematizing knowledge, and carrying out its implementation. It is not, however, the way in which our most fundamental problems are solved. Within the new research policy system, which is closely linked to strategic targets, a radical insight about a problem not on the agenda will not be pursued, thereby denying us the opportunity to exploit our inspiration. Ironically, the targeted process will lead to solutions less efficiently, because scientists will have to wait for the rarer occasions when a flash of insight happens to coincide with the externally defined target. The fact that

these coincidences do happen from time to time is used as anec-
dotal proof of the success of the new research strategy. Seen from
this perspective, the older Darwinian route to discovery appears
to remain, for now, the quickest road to successful innovation.

Martin Moskovits

NOTES

1 Nathan Rosenberg, "How the Developed Countries Became Rich,"
Daedalus 123 (Fall 1994): 127–40.
2 José Ortega, *The Revolt of the Masses* (New York: Norton, 1960).
3 Kenneth Boulding, *The Image* (Ann Arbor: University of Michigan Press,
1956).
4 Quoted in Roger Penrose, *The Emperor's New Mind* (New York: Oxford
University Press, 1989), 541.
5 Ibid.

PART I

A LABORATORY OF ONE'S OWN

JOHN CHARLES POLANYI

Nobel Prize in Chemistry, 1986

*C*hemiluminescence is the emission of *infrared radiation from the newly formed molecules of chemical reactions. When the infrared spectrometer at the University of Toronto chemistry laboratories registered the infrared chemiluminescence of hydrogen chloride molecules newly born in a chemical reaction, it marked a new beginning. For his part in pioneering work in "the development of a new field of research in chemistry — reaction dynamics — [which] has provided a much more detailed understanding of how chemical reactions take place," John Polanyi was a co-recipient of the 1986 Nobel Prize for chemistry with Dudley Herschbach and Y. T. Lee.*

Born to Hungarian parents in Berlin in 1929, Polanyi was raised and educated in England at the University of Manchester. "Chemistry was the field in which I felt at home," he said. "My father (renowned chemist and philosopher Michael Polanyi) was a chemist for a major part of his career, so the sight and smell of a chemistry laboratory was lodged in my subconscious."

Polanyi came to Canada in 1952 to do postdoctoral work at the National Research Council, before moving to Princeton in 1954 for further studies. He remains at the University of Toronto, which he joined in 1956. He currently holds the John C. Polanyi Chair in Chemistry.

Besides his work in the laboratory, Polanyi is well known as an eloquent advocate of the responsibilities of scientists to our world. He was the founding chair of the Canadian Pugwash Group in 1960, and has written many articles on science policy and the control of armaments.

Over the years, Polanyi has been awarded numerous medals and lectureships. He is a Fellow of the Royal Society of Canada, the Royal Society of London, and the U.S. National Academy of Sciences. He is also a Companion of the Order of Canada and a member of the Pontifical Academy of Science.

John Charles Polanyi

UNDERSTANDING
DISCOVERY

*M*ary Jackman, principal donor of the new chair in Chemistry, died on July 11, 1994, aged 90.★ She was a modern woman who would not, however, have objected to being called a lady. Her ideal was Virginia Woolf, author of that gentle but devastating feminist tract *A Room of One's Own*. She was given a copy by her mother in 1928, the year the book came out. There is a passage in it that sheds light on the astonishing fact that this chair is not called the Mary Rowell Jackman Chair.

> Women have served all these centuries as looking-glasses, possessing the magic and delicious power of reflecting the figure of man at twice its natural size.... How is he to go on giving judgement, civilizing natives, making laws, writing books, dressing up and speechifying at banquets, unless he can see himself at breakfast and at dinner at least twice the size he really is?

★Remarks made at gala festivities inaugurating the John C. Polanyi Chair in Chemistry.

Science is central to today's events, and science has been almost as persistently misunderstood as the female sex. The emancipation of science remains a dream. How nice it would have been if in the recent Canadian review of science policy, there had been one paper entitled "A Laboratory of One's Own." For unless our scientists are able to shelter a part of their science from the tumult of the day, they will no longer hear nature's voice, and will lose their way.

If science is to be better understood, scientists will have to find their voice. You may have read that in a test designed to determine whether computers can think, a panel of judges interrogated seven computers and seven computer scientists hidden from view. Happily, not one of the computers persuaded the judges that it was human. But quite unintentionally, five of the computer scientists misled the judges into thinking that they were computers.

No wonder that, with so little help, Virginia Woolf in *A Room of One's Own* likened scientific discovery to a shapely pebble, in contrast to a work of art that "is like a spider's web, attached ever so lightly...to life at all four corners." A pebble surely came to her mind because it was definite and not in need of creation. It simply lay there, waiting for one or another of our distinguished discoverers to trip over it.

Virginia Woolf would have welcomed the news that this view of science is nonsense. Yet for many, it is as plausible today as it was to her three-quarters of a century ago. Somehow, we must reconcile the pebble of scientific discovery with such well-known nuggets as cold fusion. The supposed facts of cold fusion — the release of nuclear energy from a glass of water — derived from observations made in several respected laboratories. How curious, then, that this pebble of truth gradually vanished. Could it be that it never was a pebble but a shimmer on Virginia Woolf's web of creation?

A scientific discovery at birth, like a story at the moment of telling, is at best 10 percent pebble and 90 percent shimmer. For a discovery to be 100 percent pebble, evidence would have to exist that admits of no doubt. That concept does not sit well with either the legal or the scientific professions.

The scientist is in the position of a lawyer trying to convince a jury of his peers that certain events, alleged to have taken place in his laboratory, establish the identity of a guilty fact. The scientist has doubts, the jury of peers has doubts, but the judge (who also has doubts) makes a ruling, good for the present. That is scientific proof. It must be, since, if science is to affect the course of history, it must influence, not an equation or a computer, but people. There is no machinery of proof that supersedes human judgment. It is because of the centrality of human judgment that we speak of the need for peer review (only occasionally, as in the case of our distinguished guest Lord Porter, does this mean going to a peer for review). We must have recourse to a judge capable of understanding the case.

Science is done by scientists, and since scientists are people, the progress of science depends more on scientific judgment than on scientific instruments. But do not, on that basis, take away our instruments. There is a limit — to embark on a new simile — to what one can paint without a brush. We may be reaching that limit. But it is certainly painting that we do, since the pebble of fact exists for us, as for any observer, only as the play of light on a partly exposed surface.

The simile of painting serves to remind us that style is involved in science. One great scientist remarked of another, whose style differed from his, that this colleague was always "lounging around, arguing about problems instead of doing experiments." The remark was made by Max Perutz, seated over there, about James Watson, who is at the next table. Watson's form of idleness, Perutz went on to say, allowed him to solve "the greatest of all biological problems: the structure of DNA." "There is more than one way of doing good science," Perutz concluded. It is a point worth bearing in mind in an age devoted to the regulation of scientific research as a means to enhance efficiency.

If the scientist, calculator in hand, is sketching a picture of the world much as does the painter, pencil in hand, then to profit from science we must support individuals who have a vision, and then give them the freedom to pursue that vision. In return, we have every right to expect a work of art, and should insist on it. But what do we do? We begin, in Canada, by labelling the pursuit of discovery as curiosity-oriented research. Curiosity is distinguished by its lack of direction. Creative effort is different. Success in creation is the reward for having a sense of direction sustained in the face of setbacks over a period of years.

Michelangelo spent four years with his head tilted back at an agonizing angle, painting a vast composite of creation on the ceiling of the Sistine Chapel. In the course of this, he made discoveries about space, colour, and form that have affected the understanding of generations. Did he paint the ceiling out of curiosity or was he possessed of a vision — together, of course, with the desire to show up Botticelli and the others who had painted the frescos below?

This blend of conviction and conceit is so far removed from curiosity as to make one wonder about policies designed for the promotion of science as a curiosity-oriented activity. Those policies are aimed at directing scientists' curiosity away from what, to the onlooker, appear to be worthless ends. If science were indeed curiosity oriented, such redirection would be cost free. But since science is sharply directed toward making discoveries, the cost of redirection is high. It is notoriously difficult to select from among unmade discoveries those that will be the most useful. That is why it is often a bad bargain to contort the tree of knowledge so that it will grow in chosen directions.

Faced with the admitted difficulty of managing the creative process, we are doubling our efforts to do so. Is this because science has failed to deliver, having given us nothing more than nuclear power, penicillin, space travel, genetic engineering, transistors, and superconductors? Or is it because governments everywhere regard as a reproach activities they cannot advantageously control? They felt that way about the marketplace for goods but, trillions of wasted dollars later, they have come to recognize the efficiency of this self-regulating system. Not so, however, with the marketplace for ideas.

What I say should not be construed as political. My reproach is directed at Charles II of England. He founded the world's first professional association of scientists, the Royal Society of London, and then proceeded to castigate its members for lack of concern about problems that mattered. He was a modest man who did not claim to know much about science, but he knew what he liked and it wasn't what the Royal Society was doing. "These gentlemen," he observed correctly, "spend their days debating nothing." They were at the time discussing vacuum which, since it is the science of empty spaces, bears, as is so often the case with new ideas, the hallmarks of frivolity. Vacuum science, as it came to be called, provided the understanding for the construction of barometers, pumps, hot air balloons, steam engines, light bulbs, vacuum tubes, thermos flasks, dried foods, neon signs, and a myriad similar delights.

Charles's ghostly presence can be felt today, mocking the mathematicians studying fractals. Their aim is to discover the mathematical equation for a leaf. Since this will come too late to be of value to God, they are being asked what earthly use it can be. Amazingly, the answer is already at hand. These equations for irregular forms are providing the basis for a new industry that transmits complex messages at low cost. But the answer to the question of utility came only after the discovery had been made, since it was only then that the question could be meaningfully posed.

It would be hard to exaggerate the resistance to this line of argument. The scientist is told that he has said the same things before, as if consistency were a fault. He is told that his picture of science, unfolding piece by piece like a cosmic jigsaw puzzle, takes insufficient account of the scarcity of public funds, as if penury were a reason for waste. He is told, most perniciously of all, that the economic crisis makes it necessary to concentrate on harvesting, not planting. That claim cries out for response.

For one of the wealthiest and most favoured nations in the world to turn its back on the sort of research represented by those gathered here today would be a betrayal of the hope that has brought so many to this country. It would be as if the early settlers, complaining of the peril of their existence, declined to map the land. The prosperity that we owe to those pioneers affords us a dazzling opportunity today to explore the vast new land of science. By exploring with daring, we shall leave a legacy that matches the one that is ours.

I have been pleading for science instead of warning against it. We are all conscious of the problems raised by science. Their very magnitude testifies to the success of science as it has been traditionally pursued. To a degree, I welcome the problems science has brought, since they require for their solution a more thoughtful world. Under pressure from modern science, we have had to reconsider the institution of war, reassess the meaning of nationhood, respect the environment, and acknowledge our obligation to the dispossessed.

Twenty-five years ago, I was one of many who fought the notion, seriously proposed, that in response to the nuclear threat we should go underground. In rejecting the proposal that we stick our heads or our entire beings in the sand, we were asserting that life is about consciousness. And that is why science, which celebrates consciousness, offers us life.

DUDLEY ROBERT HERSCHBACH

Nobel Prize in Chemistry, 1986

The crossed-beam method is a standard technique used in the field of reaction dynamics to control the ways molecules come together in a chemical reaction. One of the first crossed molecular beam instruments was constructed at the University of California at Berkeley by Dudley Herschbach in 1959. In this apparatus, two beams of molecules are accelerated and collide under known conditions. The products of the reaction are then examined by mass analysis or laser spectroscopy. The process, which earned Herschbach the 1986 Nobel Prize in chemistry with Y. T. Lee and John Polanyi, can be used to study all kinds of chemical reactions. Knowledge of the exact mechanisms of reactions will eventually give chemists better control of chemical reactions.

Herschbach, who was born in 1932 in California, researched chemical kinetics — the description of chemical reaction rates using mathematical and physical models — at Stanford University, which he attended on an academic scholarship, though he was recruited as a football player. He was certain that to understand reaction rates, he had to learn about molecular structure. This led to the study of microwave spectroscopy at Harvard University, where he earned his Ph.D.

Herschbach's description of the intimate mechanisms of numerous reactions has allowed scientists to understand them in terms of simple physical pictures. His recent work continues that tradition, but he also delves into new methods for theoretical calculation of molecular electronic structures.

Author of more than 300 research papers, Herschbach has received numerous awards, including the Linus Pauling Medal, the National Medal of Science, and the William Walker Prize. He is currently the Baird Professor of Science at Harvard, where he has been a faculty member since 1963.

Dudley Robert Herschbach

THE SHAPE OF
MOLECULAR COLLISIONS

*T*he word "shape" in my title pertains not only to molecules and their interactions. It refers also to the now vibrant state of chemical reaction dynamics, the still youthful field in which John Polanyi performs with fabled verve. Everyone knows that the *geometrical* shape of molecules has a vital role in chemistry. However, the *dynamical* shape of the interactions between molecules is just as definite and just as vital. This deals with the essence of chemistry: transforming one substance to another. Often these chemical transformations seem almost miraculous or magical. What are the molecular gymnastics that accomplish such feats? I became intrigued with this question early on.

Soon after I arrived at college, I brashly asked my freshman adviser, Harold Johnston, about his "research," something I had just learned that university professors did. He described his studies of chemical reactions and explained the difficulties in unravelling how they take place. In those days, chemists had to proceed by concocting a list of postulated steps in which some molecule begets another one or two that in turn beget others. Johnston emphasized that this was always a guessing game; there was no way to test such schemes definitively. You couldn't be sure you had included all the steps. The most interesting species were extremely reactive intermediates that didn't stay around, so could not be directly observed. I was impressed that chemists doggedly persisted in trying to divine reaction pathways despite such daunting handicaps.

Only four years later, an offhand remark by a physics professor showed me how individual reaction steps and intermediate species might be directly observed. The professor mentioned an experiment in the 1920s carried out by Otto Stern to measure the distribution of molecular speeds. In an evacuated glass tube a few inches long, Stern evaporated silver atoms from a hot wire. The atoms passed through collimating slits to form a ribbon-like beam, which then traversed a rotating device that enabled him to determine how fast the atoms were travelling. I immediately contacted Hal Johnston, with the naive notion that chemical reactions could be studied by crossing two such molecular beams in a vacuum to isolate single collisions and directly detect the products. He laughed and said, "Well, sure, of course, but there's not enough intensity." It did look difficult. Molecular beam methods had found many applications in physics, but, as of the early 1950s, very little had been done in studying molecular collisions because that required means to detect products at extremely low levels.

For instance, in the early crossed-beam experiments my students and I undertook at Berkeley in 1960, the yield of product corresponded to only a monolayer of molecules per month. Nonetheless, as I'll describe, it proved feasible to study such reactions in considerable detail and ultimately others with far smaller yields. First, however, I will give more background for this work.

After our initial crude experiments at Berkeley, I was asked to give a talk in the physics department. I began by praising the legacy of Otto Stern that had inspired our work and so much else. Surprisingly, that seemed to cause some professors in the front row to giggle. Afterwards, one of them asked me if I knew that Stern was in the audience. I was amazed, but indeed I had noticed a little man sitting far back by himself. He looked rather like Charlie Chaplin, dressed all in black and wearing a Homburg hat. After retiring a few years before, Stern had moved to Berkeley. I later became acquainted with him and had the chance to hear some instructive stories about his early work. I will retell just one, dealing with his experiment to measure the distribution of molecular speeds. He said that at the outset, he did not doubt the theoretical prediction, yet there had been no other means to confirm it and he wanted to provide a direct experimental test. Stern found that his data showed a systematic deviation from the theoretical curve, but he sent off a preliminary manuscript to some colleagues. One promptly responded, pointing out that an extra factor was needed because the atoms passed through a slit on the way to the detector. This extra factor arises from a familiar effect: if people were now to dash for the exit, the faster ones would get there sooner. When Stern took account of this biasing factor, sure enough the theory agreed much better with experiment. Gleefully, he added, "That letter came from Albert Einstein."

Under ordinary chemical conditions, molecules interact in great, unruly mobs. I must emphasize how tiny molecules are and how wildly they careen about in typical circumstances. To repeat a favourite comparison: the number of molecules in a teaspoon of water is roughly the same as the number of teaspoons of water in all the world's oceans. Another favourite example: suppose a minuscule bug were to creep across your fingernail at a very sedate pace, so slowly that it takes a year to do so. At that rate, the bug would pass by a molecule in just one second.

A similar estimate was given by Lord Rayleigh, who determined the size of a molecule for the first time only in 1892, using a method invented by Benjamin Franklin in 1773. Curious about the spreading of oil on water, Franklin had tossed some olive oil on a pond and was astounded to observe that half a teaspoon quickly spread over about half an acre. By carefully repeating the experiment in his Victorian bathtub, Rayleigh obtained a quantitative measure of the size of an olive oil molecule from the ratio of the volume of oil to the area of the film formed by it.

Tiny as they are, molecules move extremely fast, typically with the speed of rifle bullets. They zip about every which way, with a broad range of speeds, and also tumble freely with random spatial orientations. They continually collide with each other, bouncing off in all directions. This chaotic lifestyle is the basic problem if we want to find out what happens in the chemical interactions that make and break bonds. The molecular beam methods introduced by Stern have enabled us to impose more orderly behaviour.

Figure 1, inspired by a visit to Canada some years ago, shows that molecular beams should be readily intelligible to hockey fans. As a rough analogy, the top cartoon shows two streams of blind-folded hockey players about to cross paths. Actually, if molecules were magnified to the size of people, the spacing between them in our beams would typically be about 30 metres, much larger than in the cartoon. Furthermore, such a magnified scale would show our beam molecules forming a stream 30 kilometres wide, or more, not proceeding in single file. When two such dilute molecular streams cross, most molecules undergo only grazing collisions and are only slightly deviated from their original path. Occasionally, a hard collision of the sort seen in hockey does occur. Those can be drastic indeed; a chemical reaction switches limbs or torsos between the molecular players. With suitable detectors, we can observe the direction and velocity of the recoiling product molecules, as well as how rapidly they are tumbling and how vigorously their atomic limbs are vibrating. That tells us a great deal about the forces governing the reactive collisions.

Early crossed-beam experiments were of necessity limited to a special family of reactions that was particularly amenable. These reactions had exceptionally large product yields that could be measured by means of a remarkably simple, sensitive, and specific detector. That was crucial since, as noted above, under crossed-beam conditions the flux of products arriving at the detector corresponded to only a monolayer of molecules per month. For

FIGURE 1 *Hockey analogy for interaction of two beams of molecules intersecting within a vacuum. Most will miss or have only grazing collisions; a few will smack hard into one another. Measuring the direction and speed of the rebounding collision partners provides incisive information about the forces exerted in the encounter.*

these special reactions, it was feasible to use as a detector just a hot filament, like that in an incandescent light bulb. This exploited an unusual property of the product molecules, which give up an electron to the hot filament and evaporate from it as positively charged ions. These ion currents were readily measurable even for a very low flux of products. Just as important, the detector was entirely unresponsive to the much greater background flux of other species, such as the pump oil molecules wandering about in the imperfect vacuum provided by our rudimentary apparatus.

The special reactions, so essential for the early beam experiments, were among a large family explored in the 1920s by John Polanyi's father, Michael. He carried out the first systematic study of how chemical structures affected chemical reactivity. Figure 2

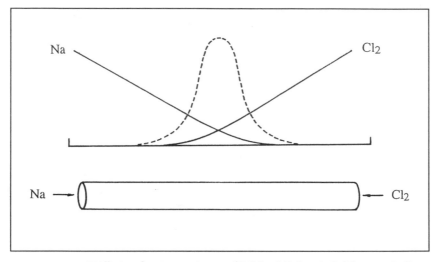

FIGURE 2 *Diffusion flame experiment of Michael Polanyi. Solid curves indicate concentrations of the reactant species, Na and Cl_2, as they diffuse into inert gas in the reaction tube. Dashed curve indicates distribution of the NaCl produced in the reaction.*

depicts one of his typical experiments. He had a small glass tube containing an inert gas, usually argon, at low pressure. He allowed sodium vapour to diffuse into one end of the tube and chlorine molecules into the other end. Where the joint concentration of the reactants peaked, about midway down the tube, reaction produced a deposit of sodium chloride salt. From the width of the salt deposit, compared with the known rate of diffusion through argon, he could determine with fair accuracy how rapidly the reaction occurred. There were also subsidiary reactions of great interest that generated light, so his method was called a diffusion flame. In a book Michael Polanyi published in 1932, the year I was born, he shows one of his graduate students reading a paper by the light of this diffusion flame. Thirty years later, it proved to be a beacon illuminating the way for young chemists eager to probe reaction dynamics with molecular beams.

The historical development offers lessons that deserve emphasis. In the early days, when the chemical scope of molecular beams was severely limited, there were three schools of thought. There was what soon came to be called the lunatic fringe, John Polanyi among them, who were excited and optimistic. There were the wise people, mostly more senior, who were pessimistic because of the intensity problem. And there were sceptics who, quite reasonably, felt that although beam studies were finding interesting results for a few very special reactions, the accessible family was far too small and eccentric to be of any general interest.

In retrospect, what happened seems characteristic of many new fields destined to be fruitful. The prospects opened up by early results were greatly amplified by attracting extremely able and enterprising people, and also by exploiting tools provided by unanticipated developments in other fields. The opportunity to examine chemistry at the level of single collisions appealed to many graduate students, postdoctoral fellows, and young faculty who wanted to undertake something reckless. This sparked much new theoretical work as well as many other experimental efforts. The evangelical fervour of the lunatic fringe grew rapidly, even though up until 1968 crossed-beam studies remained limited to the special family of alkali atom reactions.

Indeed we found unexpected variety in the dynamics for reactions with different target molecules. In some reactions, the reagents execute a folk dance, lingering together long enough to rotate completely around several times before the products whirl away. For such cases, the angular distribution of the products resembles that for water sprayed from a lawn sprinkler. Other reactive encounters are very brisk. In some, the incident alkali atom swoops in and almost surreptitiously plucks a halogen atom from the target molecule, which continues on its way as if unaware of the theft. Still other brisk reactions are brutal encounters involving strong repulsive forces. In these, the products are flung backwards at high velocities, recalling an old advertisement that described Rice Krispies as the cereal "shot from guns." Mapping out all this dynamical variety enabled us to learn how the system was governed by simple features of the electronic structure of the reactant molecule.

Such understanding in terms of electronic structure is the "Holy Grail" for chemical dynamics. Obtaining it for alkali reactions was gratifying, even if these were thought to be unrepresentative. Yet, of course, we wanted to extend beam studies to a wider range of reactions. Some attempts by other researchers had reinforced an unduly pessimistic view of the prospects. However, in 1967, just as we were ready to try to go "beyond the alkali age," an experimental genius joined my laboratory as a postdoctoral fellow. He was Yuan Lee, who I like to call the Mozart of chemical physics. Classical musicians especially admire Mozart for his skill in making optimal use of minimal material. Likewise, in scientific experiments heavily dependent on instrumentation, it is vital to make things only as complicated as they need to be, not more so. Otherwise, too many things can go wrong. Led by Yuan, we were able to construct a new beam apparatus with a mass spectrometric detector of remarkable sensitivity and selectivity. I would like to mention some instructive aspects of this detector.

How to discriminate against unwanted background is the key problem. Most molecules in the crossed-beam method do not react where the two diffuse beams intersect, so the molecules continue on and bounce off the apparatus walls somewhere, just as hockey players rebound from the sides of an ice rink. Eventually many of these molecules form the same product in the background that we want to observe in the beam. This background threatens the basic aim of the experiment: to observe the freshly formed product molecules from reactions that occur in single collisions at the intersection zone of the crossed beams. We were able to defeat the background in two ways. One involved a specially designed nested pumping scheme. The other is of more philosophical interest.

The product molecules that reach the innermost sanctum of our mass spectrometer are bombarded there by electrons to turn some

molecules into the ions we detect. However, this process is ineffi-
cient; only about one of each 10,000 product molecules is ionized.
We want the other 9,999 un-ionized molecules to depart the
premises without disturbing anything. If these molecules instead
encounter a wall (as in designs tried elsewhere), many may be
ionized after bouncing off the wall. That creates a prohibitively
high noise level at the heart of the detector. To avoid such noise,
we simply provided an exit hole to allow the un-ionized molecules to fly out of the electron bombardment region without
impediment. The philosophical lesson, applicable well beyond
science, is that often it is more important to reduce noise than to
enhance the signal itself. In demanding experiments of all kinds,
simple but essential things can make an enormous difference.

This mass spectrometric detector, later used by many laboratories, enabled study of a wide range of reactions. A striking aspect
soon emerged: many dynamical features of other reactions and
some electronic aspects could be readily understood in terms
of what we had already learned from the alkali atom reactions.
Figure 3 illustrates this situation. The reaction of hydrogen atoms
with chlorine molecules to form hydrogen chloride served as the
prototype in the development of John Polanyi's beautiful method
of chemiluminescence. The product hydrogen chloride molecule
glows faintly, emitting infrared photons that reveal its vibrational
and rotational motions and thus provide much information about
the forces in the reaction. This is complementary to the dynamical information we obtained by observing the distribution in
angle and translational velocity of the hydrogen chloride. Quite
unexpectedly, we found that a contour map of the product distribution in angle and velocity turned out to be virtually identical,
except for scale, to the map for the first alkali reaction we had
studied years before. That involved potassium atoms reacting with
methyl iodide to form potassium iodide. The kinship with the
hydrogen atom plus chlorine reaction proved to be explicable in
terms of electronic structure. This connection brought out a new
perspective, in which the alkali reaction family no longer appears
unrepresentative.

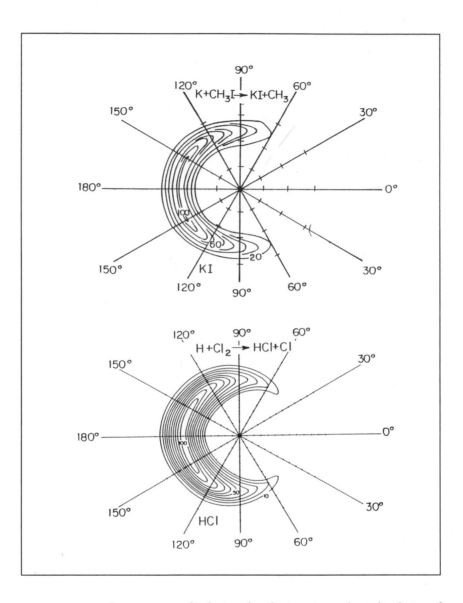

FIGURE 3 *Contour maps displaying distributions in angle and velocity of KI product from K + CH₃I reaction (top) and HCl product from H + Cl₂ reaction (bottom). Angular scale indicates direction (same for 0°, opposite for 180°) in which the product molecules emerge relative to the incident reactant atom beam (K or H). Tick marks along radial lines indicate velocity intervals of 200 meters/second. Contours show intensity relative to peak (100%).*

Many other experimental developments, especially supersonic beam techniques and laser spectroscopy, now greatly enhance our ability to probe the intimate dynamics of molecular collisions. I will describe some impressionistic aspects. Figure 4 contrasts two modes of producing a molecular beam. We consider a small source chamber within a vacuum apparatus. The canonical physics literature, going back to Otto Stern, stressed that the pressure within the source chamber should be kept low enough so that molecules, as they emerge from the exit orifice, do not collide with each other. In this realm of "effusive" or "molecular" flow, the emergent beam provides a true random sample of the gas within the source, undistorted by collisions. Of course, this canonical ideal was blatantly violated by chemists who wanted to study reactions in crossed beams. Since such studies desperately needed intensity, much higher source pressures were used. Collisions within the orifice then produce supersonic flow. This has other advantageous properties. Supersonic beams have narrow distributions in both direction and molecular speeds. Also, the rotational and vibrational temperatures of the molecules can be very low, whereas seeding heavy molecules in a large excess of light diluent

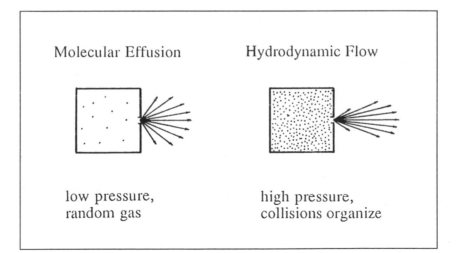

Molecular Effusion   Hydrodynamic Flow

low pressure,   high pressure,
random gas   collisions organize

FIGURE 4   *Contrast between production of a molecular beam by effusion (at left) or by a supersonic expansion (at right).*

gas provides an easy way to accelerate the molecules to high translational energies.

These properties of supersonic beams, all resulting from collisions as molecules crowd out the exit aperture, are readily understood by Bostonians, but may be less apparent to Torontonians, who are much more polite. A famous Boston department store, Filene's, regularly has Saturday morning sales. Typically, a dense crowd gathers (like the high-pressure gas within the beam source). When the doors are thrown open and the crowd rushes in, collisions induce everybody to flow in the same direction with the same speed whether they want to or not. Moreover, if some customers are excited at the prospect of a bargain and leap about or turn handstands (like vibrating or rotating molecules), they suffer more collisions — even black eyes and bloody noses. Thereby such lively customers are calmed down (just as molecular vibration and rotation can be cooled to very low effective temperatures). If a busload of highly kinetic children is turned loose, however, collisions can accelerate the adults to higher velocities (as happens when heavy molecules are seeded in an expanding light gas). The upshot is that, in supersonic expansions, collisions organize the molecular beam far better than we could manage to do by any mechanical means.

To conclude this impressionistic sampling, I will skip to recent work that aims to achieve more incisive resolution of molecular collision dynamics. Even under the single-collision conditions provided by crossed beams, we must average over a "dartboard" distribution of impacts as well as over random rotational orientations of the tumbling target molecule. To use another sports metaphor: unlike a baseball pitcher, we cannot grab an individual atom and fling it at a target molecule, low and inside one time, high and outside the next. Instead, we send a diffuse stream of molecules, very broad compared with their size, to intersect another stream. The chance that any particular molecule in one beam hits more than one in the other beam is entirely negligible, but we have no control over where it collides. It is as if we throw many balls at once, but the batter only gets to swing at one. The information that is lost because we cannot control where our molecular ball arrives at the batter was long thought to be irretrievable.

Without going into detail, I can tell you there is a way to get equivalent information. Since we cannot throw the pitch where we want over the plate, we act instead like the umpire and call where it went. More precisely, we find out where the pitch was when it was struck by the batter. This can be done by determining simultaneously the direction and speed of flight of the product molecule and how it is rotating in space. The latter can be found by exciting the molecule with laser light and observing the fluorescence emission. The excited molecule acts like a tiny rotating radio antenna; it emits light with a pattern that reveals the orientation of its rotation axis.

Another approach is required to cope with the random orientations and tumbling of the target molecules. In the cartoon of figure 2, the streams of hockey players really should be tumbling head-over-heels. For typical molecules, the peripheral velocity of rotation is comparable to the speed of a jet aircraft. Again, except for special situations, this random tumbling was long thought to be unquenchable. But averaging over it appreciably degrades the resolution of collision dynamics. Figure 5 indicates a simple

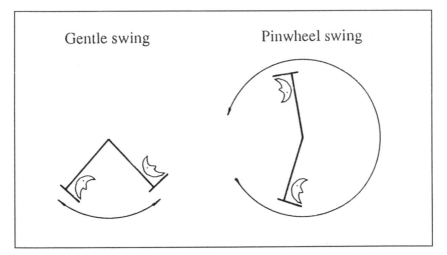

FIGURE 5 *Gymnastic analogy for method or orienting molecules.*

solution that was recently demonstrated to be feasible in practice. This pertains to molecules that interact appreciably with an external electric or magnetic field. Ordinarily, even for the largest field strengths that can be maintained in a beam apparatus, the rapid tumbling of the molecule drastically weakens the interaction. Then the molecules do not become appreciably oriented in the field, but simply continue pinwheeling. However, by means of a supersonic expansion, we can make the rotational temperature of the molecules very low, within a degree or so of absolute zero. The tumbling is then languid, so in a strong field a molecule can no longer pinwheel. Rather, it swings to and fro about the field direction like a tiny pendulum, and thus is oriented in space. This is analogous to a child on a swing going gently back and forth in the Earth's gravitational field rather than recklessly gyrating.

My chief aim here has been to sketch how our ability to learn about the dynamics of molecular collisions has taken shape. I lingered fondly on some of the early episodes because, as in dynamics generally, the initial conditions are often as important as the prevailing forces. I hope that students and young researchers might be encouraged to see how simple and naive were the first steps. I hope also that officials responsible for support of science might better appreciate how crucial a long-range view is, for fundamental work that strives to open up new vistas. Most of the frontier we are now exploring could not, at the outset, even be glimpsed. That is still the case in many areas that young recruits to science will soon be pursuing.

In this wider context, I am glad to acknowledge that the choice of my title was prompted by Professor Polly Windsor of Toronto. She wrote a fascinating book about the history of zoological science at Harvard, entitled *Reading the Shape of Nature*. Since the study of esoteric molecular encounters, like that of bizarre fossils, may seem remote from practical concerns, I want to close by addressing that question. In response, I offer a metaphor and a parable.

The metaphor is implicit in Windsor's poetic title for her book. Nature speaks to us in many tongues. They are all alien.

The task of the scientist pursuing "curiosity-driven" research is to try to discover something of the vocabulary and the grammar of one or more of these languages. To the extent that the scientist succeeds, we gain the ability to decipher many messages that nature has left for us, blithely or coyly. No matter how much human effort and money we might invest to solve a practical problem in science or technology, failure is inevitable unless we can read the answers that nature is willing to give us. The basic research that provides such understanding is the most practical investment we can make.

The parable is an unfinished story about unexpected linkages. It involves supersonic molecular beams, fireplace soot, unidentified interstellar spectra, and catastrophic disease. Everyone has heard about the discovery a few years ago of molecules composed of sixty carbon atoms, shaped like a soccer ball and whimsically named "Bucky-balls" to celebrate their architectural resemblance to Buckminster Fuller's geodesic domes. The first evidence for these molecules came from experiments using supersonic beams to generate clusters of carbon atoms. The drastic cooling in the supersonic expansion fostered formation of clusters with a wide range in size. Among them, the sixty-atom cluster appeared to be especially stable. To account for this, the researchers speculated that the molecules might have the highly symmetrical soccer-ball structure.

Further study by other scientists was stimulated by the question of whether carbon clusters might be responsible for an extensive series of absorption lines seen in interstellar spectra. The origin of these lines has been a mystery for more than eighty years. Although carbon clusters do not seem to be the answer, the work motivated by this mystery led to the discovery that Bucky-balls could be extracted in quantity from soot. That has opened up to synthetic chemists a vast new world of molecular structures, built with a form of carbon that has sixty valences rather than just four. By looking at the heavens, scientists came to find, in ashes that had lain under the feet of ancestral cavemen, a Cinderella-like molecule.

Our parable continues at a computer screen. Two years ago, a graduate student at the University of California at San Francisco was to see if he could design or find a molecule that would inactivate an enzyme that is crucial for replication of the AIDS virus. The inactivating model needs to have the right size and shape to fit into a cleft in the enzyme. The molecule also needs to present a water-repellent torso, since the cleft is hydrophobic. The student's girlfriend, listening to him lament that what he had tried did not fit, teasingly suggested that he try a Bucky-ball. He went back to the computer and found it was just right.

Soon a chemist at the University of California at Santa Barbara synthesized a derivative of carbon-sixty which has a pair of wings that make the molecule water-soluble, despite its hydrophobic torso. Physiologists at Emory University in Georgia then found that, at least in a test tube, this Bucky-ball derivative does indeed totally inactivate the enzyme that governs replication of the AIDS virus.

This is still a long way from having an actual AIDS drug that can function in living cells. However, like many other scientific parables, the story serves to emphasize that basic research inevitably creates unforeseen opportunities. Otto Stern could not have imagined that his curiosity about the form of a molecular velocity distribution might ultimately merge with many other efforts to contend with a deadly virus. Grateful for such a heritage, we can now imagine much more, as we seek to read the shape of nature.

CHARLES HARD TOWNES

Nobel Prize in Physics, 1964

*M*asers, *an acronym for microwave amplification by stimulated emission of radiation, are the forerunners of lasers. Like lasers, they produce intense, highly coherent radiation with a narrow band of wavelengths. The radiation beam from lasers and masers does not diverge with distance as much as it does with incandescent light sources, making them ideal for use in telecommunications systems. Charles Townes received the Nobel Prize in physics in 1964 "for fundamental work in the field of quantum electronics, which has led to the construction of oscillators and amplifiers based on the maser-laser principle." The first maser was also independently discovered by Nikolai Basov and Alexander Prochorov, with whom he shared the prize.*

Born in South Carolina in 1915, Townes graduated from Furman University with a B.A. in modern languages and a B.S. in physics at the age of nineteen. He received his masters from Duke University and his Ph.D. from the California Institute of Technology in 1939. It was during the war, while designing radar systems at Bell Laboratories, that he developed his interest in microwave spectroscopy, an interest he pursued at Columbia University.

Albert Einstein first described stimulated emission, but this process was considered theoretical and not practically usable until Townes demonstrated the first working model of a maser in 1954. The maser was used in satellite transmission systems. Its success ignited the search for lasers that could operate in the higher frequencies of infrared, and ultimately in the visible and ultraviolet light. Lasers are now used everywhere from supermarket checkouts to hospital operating rooms.

Townes's work for the past twenty years has been primarily in astrophysics at the University of California, where he has been since 1967. His research has yielded such developments as new infrared techniques, discovery of stable molecules in galactic clouds, and evidence for a large black hole in the centre of our galaxy.

Charles Hard Townes

UNPREDICTABILITY
IN SCIENCE
AND TECHNOLOGY

Science is the systematic use of exploration and reason to understand our universe and ourselves. Despite the number of refined explanations of science and the scientific method, the field is not easily defined. I like the interpretation given by another Nobel laureate in physics and quasi-philosopher, Percy Bridgeman, who said, "Scientific method: to work like the devil to get the answer with no holds barred." It is a human endeavour with many high-precision aspects, but it can also be elusive and indefinable.

Science has a multiplex of values. We typically talk about basic and applied science, although they are not totally separate. The value of basic science on the one hand is cultural; it satisfies human curiosity, our sense of exploration; it gives us a different perspective on life and what we and our universe are all about. Just think of what astronomy does to the sense of our own magnitude compared with what is out there. Or the fact that we have all come from a single cell. There are many factors and aspects of science that affect our perspective and attitudes towards life, and satisfy the natural curiosity in humans that is so evident in young children and that we hope goes on throughout life. The cultural value of science is satisfying to humans.

Applied or practical values are those values we think of as affecting our living and how we function. They can also be very satisfying. By understanding how things work, we can somewhat control them, thereby influencing our potential and our way of life. While society may support the ideas and the cultural aspects of science as well as those of music or art, governmental support for science is primarily reasoned as a support for those things that can improve our living conditions. It is applied science that the government and politicians generally think of as science — science that is done for specific reasons. They acknowledge the need for basic science, but primarily in terms of what it can accomplish in the applied realm. How we determine those areas of science that we choose to support is a crucial process we should all be concerned about.

Science and technology can bring about changes within a decade or so. Young people can expect to see profound changes in their lifetime. No one knows now what they will be — making it difficult to plan for them — but they will take place, and science will play a major role in producing them. How can we devise a plan to accomplish important tasks if we do not know where the changes will be? A look ahead reveals nothing very clearly about presently unknown and new discoveries. Contrary to what most people believe, scientists do not possess the ability to predict the future, despite their intensive knowledge.

Lord Kelvin, one of Great Britain's great scientists at the end of the last century, said that radio had no future; heavier-than-air flying machines were impossible; and x-rays were a hoax. Lord Rayleigh, another remarkable British scientist of the same period, said, "I have not the smallest molecule of faith in aerial navigation other than ballooning." A few years later, in 1903, the Wright brothers were flying.

Nor is common knowledge more perspicacious. In 1909 the popular journal *Scientific American*, trying to understand science and its future, carried this quotation: "The automobile has practically reached the limit of its development." Certainly some of the automobile's structure is the same today as it was in 1909, but no one will dispute that changes have been made.

Somewhat later Robert Millikan, perhaps the most outstanding physicist of his generation in the United States, spoke in 1929 about the wild notion of getting energy out of nuclei. He said, "The energy available through disintegration of radioactive or any other atoms may perhaps be sufficient to keep the corner peanut and popcorn man going in our larger cities for a long time, but that's all." Lord Rutherford, one of the most important physicists of his day in Europe and head of the Cavendish Laboratories, where neutrons were discovered and the first artificial radioactivity was produced, also mentioned nuclear prospects in a talk in New York in 1933. He said, "Anyone who expects a source of power from the transformation of these atoms is talking moonshine." The *New York Times*, looking for some reaction, interviewed a number of other famous American scientists, all of whom expressed delight that Rutherford had pointed out the futility of such expectations. Only one prominent scientist, a young man named E. O. Lawrence, who was beginning to be known because of his invention of the cyclotron, disagreed with Rutherford. He said that although he did not know how it could be done, he still believed there might be a way. It was only a few years later, in 1939, that fission came along, and every physics graduate student immediately speculated that, since there was obviously a great deal of energy released in that process, we should be able to use it.

People in business, practical people who are responsible for long-term planning, have also been off the mark in predicting the future. Thomas Watson, founder of IBM, said in 1943, "I think there's a world market for about five computers." As recently as 1977, Ken Olson, head of Digital Equipment or DEC and a great technical leader, said, "There is no reason for any individual to have a computer in his home." Astronomer Royal Richard Woolley said in 1956, "Space travel is utter bilge." One year later, *Sputnik* was up. Obviously these were not ignorant people; it's the problem that is difficult. When they talk so conclusively about certain things, their reasoning — although tight — is based on what is recognized at the time. But there are other aspects of technology besides the requirements or ideas of the moment that are not easy to recognize before their time. Watson was basing his statement about computers on what computers were like in 1943.

Scientists can be overoptimistic as well as pessimistic. In 1956 John Von Neumann, one of the world's greatest applied mathematicians, said, "A few decades hence, energy may be free, just like unmetered air." He was thinking of fusion and the possibility that, someday, energy will be abundant and easy, extracted from a bathtub of water.

Many of the changes from misapprehension to the realization of that misapprehension take no longer than a decade. This short time scale poses a decision-making problem for politicians, businesspeople, and society in general. The time for a change in knowledge or perspective is often relatively short, perhaps ten years, but the actual time for it to become an important industrial or economic effect is more like twenty years, too long a period for most planning schedules. Neither politicians nor businesspeople last so long. They cannot claim to know what the future holds, and they hesitate to spend money for what will be new fifteen or twenty years hence. Neither they, nor anyone else, would know what to do. At the same time, we know there will be an increase in knowledge and understanding which produces new results that require planning. This is our paradox.

The importance of change and new ideas is one reason we do not generally allow monolithic industries controlled by one person or group. Instead, we encourage competition. But, as a result, most industries in the United States have steadily decreased long-term research in their laboratories for economic reasons. They must compete with companies that are not doing research.

Whom does that leave to foster research? Society and government must support these longer-term activities.

It has been suggested that if knowledgeable people put their heads together and came to a careful consensus about how best to foster industry and economic growth, we might get some right answers on how and what to plan. President Franklin Roosevelt tried that in 1937. He asked a commission to advise the government on what would be the most important technical and industrial developments for the United States in the next twenty-five years so that he could support them properly. The commissioners came out with a fairly sensible report, citing agricultural research as important because it could improve crop yields, and recommending the improvement of rotating machinery for more efficiency. They also said that synthetic gasoline would become important, perhaps because the Germans were already making it. That, obviously, has not become true. What they were doing was extending what they already knew and what was more or less under way already.

It is important to consider the things they missed. They missed antibiotics completely, even though they had already been discovered by Alexander Fleming; Howard Florey put them to more practical use just a year later. They missed jet aircraft. They missed rockets and space exploration. They missed radar. They missed computer development. They missed the transistor. They missed the laser, which became important within twenty-five years. They missed genetic engineering, which also came along approximately within that time frame. What they missed were all the most exciting breakthroughs and the most potent changes. The commission, made up of senior scientists, engineers, and intelligent people, made very sensible extrapolations of what they knew. But the scientific and technical plans that we make for the future must reflect the fact that the future is largely unknown to us.

As a monopoly, the Bell Telephone System in the United States was able to support a laboratory for a long time, using rates which were established with government permission, but which could be justified as being reasonable. The Bell Telephone Laboratories, founded in 1920, was the most impressive industrial laboratory in the United States. Between 1935 and 1965, long-distance telephone costs to the user in the United States went down by a factor of four in actual dollars, a factor of twelve taking inflation into account. Over these thirty years of communication, the cost went down almost solely due to research and development in the Bell Laboratories. From its beginning up to 1965, the laboratories had cost the company $2 billion. Every year, the resulting savings on long-distance calls were more than ten times as much as the total cost of the laboratories. Not all of the laboratories' work was successful, but much of it was, and it resulted in big changes. It is important for science and technology to be able to continue such performances. For this, we must develop insightful research policies.

The decisions on what research to support were difficult even for the Bell Laboratories. Back in the 1930s Mervyn Kelly, director of research at the laboratories, was aware that solid-state physics was becoming an accepted field. He started hiring good solid-state physicists, with the rationale that the new field must be important to a company dealing with materials, wires, and resistors. He hired Bill Shockley and Walter Brattain. Shortly after the war, Bell Lab-oratories managed to hire John Bardeen. Many people think Kelly foresaw the transistor, but I believe that is not the case. He simply recognized the likely importance of the new solid-state physics. In about 1942, while at Bell Laboratories, Shockley thought he had found a way to make an amplifier with solids, using a semiconductor. He was extremely disappointed when he got someone to try out his invention, and the amplifier didn't work. He told me he didn't understand it, but he had to give up the idea.

The transistor really was discovered by accident. Brattain was studying surface phenomenon on semiconductors and he witnessed a peculiar effect as he conducted current through a surface contact. He talked to Bardeen, who, being a good theorist, explained it. They had amplification. Shockley, who was away in Europe, rushed back to work on it. He added some other ideas, and we had the transistor in several forms — by accident, yes, but also by a sort of planning: by getting the right people in the right field. Many other people had to work on the transistor to make it useful to the telephone company, but the transistor had emerged.

There were also cases, such as the laser, where Bell's policies were not quite as wise. The laser developed out of a study of the absorption of microwaves in molecules, which in turn came about because of the interaction between applied and fundamental work on radar developments during the war. After the war, we had radar equipment and oscillators in the microwave region, and I had recognized that water could absorb these radar waves. That made one of the radars useless because the wrong wavelength had been chosen, one that encountered water vapor absorption in moist air. This was of considerable interest to me and others, and marked the beginning of work in microwave spectroscopy, where we were able to make many interesting spectroscopic studies of molecules. Such work started in industrial laboratories, because they had the equipment and the experienced people. Unfortunately, industrial laboratories also shut it down, failing to see how it could have any further use for them.

Excellent laboratories — General Electric, Westinghouse, RCA — all vetoed work in microwave spectroscopy. At Bell Laboratories, they were glad to have me work in that field because they thought it was good physics, but microwave spectroscopy was not pertinent enough to their business goals. When I got an offer from Columbia University I took it, to be able to continue work in microwave spectroscopy in an environment where other people were interested in the field.

My objective at Columbia was to study molecules and atoms. As I decreased the wavelength, the effects got more and more powerful and more interesting. We could get down to a few millimetres' wavelength, but we wanted to go even shorter. One day, sitting on a park bench in Washington, D.C., frustrated by hard work but lack of progress, it suddenly occurred to me to use molecules and atoms as sources of microwaves because of their resonances.

My intention was to use molecular beams to provide a means of generating short waves, so I found a student who had done undergraduate work in that area, Jim Gordon, and told him I thought an attempt to build an oscillator based on stimulated emission of radiation from molecules would make a good thesis. Three years later he had the device going, which we christened a maser for microwave amplification by stimulated emission of radiation. No one was very interested and no one tried to duplicate it. When we explained the idea before we actually demonstrated its potential, the only reaction we got was lukewarm interest. I was urged during that time to work on magnetrons, because the laboratory was supported by the military and they wanted development in that area. I wasn't interested. I was doing something that did not interest people in applied science, the sources of money, but I enjoyed it and I believed the maser would work.

The success of the maser and development of the field depended on the interaction between science and technology. I had worked on radar during the war, and the ideas I used were a combination of engineering and physics. Physicists knew the principles involved, but they liked to think of electromagnetic radiation in terms of photons, and they were concerned about the uncertainty principle. I had substantial arguments with physicists who didn't believe my ideas were right. They reasoned that there would not be coherent radiation because of the uncertainty principle. Engineers, who knew about continuous waves and coherent oscillators, had never heard of stimulated emission — stimulating a molecule with a wave to give up its energy to that wave exactly in phase and coherent with it — which was one of the requirements of the maser and which physicists knew about.

The interconnection within science of seemingly unconnected ideas is also important. In this particular case, I was using a molecular beam because I was familiar with molecular beams and because I had access to the laboratory at Columbia where a great deal of such work had been done. Just a month before, I had heard a lecture by a German scientist, Wolfgang Paul, on a special quadrupole focuser that proved to be important. Also, I am sure I was aware of work on negative temperatures that had been done at Harvard. Ideas from other people contributed, and further development of the field was based on multiple contributions.

The interplay between universities and industry was also important in this development. Industry had hired many of the people in microwave and radiospectroscopy, fields that had grown out of applied work during the war but had then been developed in the universities. All industrial laboratories, including Bell's, had abandoned their interest in microwave and radio spectroscopy, but when the masers began to develop, they came back to it. Bell Laboratories quickly hired Jim Gordon and Art Schawlow. Later, Schawlow and I extended the maser idea to amplify light, hense the laser or light amplification by stimulated emission of radiation. Schawlow took our idea to Bell's patent attorneys. They told him that light was never of any importance to communication, but agreed to patent it, somewhat unenthusiastically, after we proposed a way of communicating with light from a laser. Soon, Bell Laboratories and others became more enthusiastic. Industry took over and, essentially, all the lasers and the new inventions since have been done in industry, including the first operating system made at Hughes, the He Ne system of the Bell Laboratories and the semiconductor laser invented in General Electric laboratories.

Looking back, I feel like the beaver talking to his friend the rabbit at the bottom of the big Hoover Dam in the Grand Canyon. This is a magnificent structure and a remarkable human achievement. The beaver looks at it and says to the rabbit, "I didn't really build that dam all myself, but it's based on an idea of mine." That's the same with the laser. All kinds of people have made important contributions.

One might compare the growth of technology to chaos. The weather is based on complex phenomena where little perturbations can build up into big changes. It is hard to predict what will happen when the energy from the Sun interacts with the Earth's atmosphere and surface. It is said that a flap of a butterfly's wing in China can eventually end up in a big storm on the Atlantic. We can predict the weather over a short period of time, but not over a long period. We know that we will have a few big storms in winter, a few very hot days in summer, but we cannot know exactly how many. Scientific discoveries follow that same pattern.

We don't know exactly what research will pay off, what will build up, but we do know, historically, that important discoveries will occur and that they will have a major effect on technology and business.

I am reminded of the continuity of human experience by a quotation I recently came across. "The budget should be balanced, the treasury should be refilled, public debt should be reduced, the arrogance of officialdom should be tempered and controlled, and the assistance to foreign lands should be curtailed lest Rome become bankrupt." That was Cicero in 63 B.C. Things change, but they remain the same. To predict the future of science and technology, the past is our evidence.

Pure and applied science are inseparable and can only grow together. If our research in applied science is not solid, we cannot continue to do solid research in pure science and vice versa. When Robert Millikan did his experiment measuring the charge on the electron, he built a thousand lead cells with his own hands. We can now pick something that will do the equivalent off the shelf. What industry and technology produce is extremely important in extending further developments in basic research.

Astronomer Martin Harwit has said that most significant discoveries in astronomy have been made shortly after a new technique has been introduced, generally by people outside the field. To some extent, that is true of every field. As an example, let me note some of the most basic discoveries that came out of interest in applied work. Consider the study of noise. Bell Laboratories asked a physicist engineer named J.B. Johnson to study the noise in circuits and devise a way to control it. He discovered what is now known as Johnson noise, a fundamental noise in resistors which is always there. It was discovered by an attempt to find where noise comes from. Bell asked another engineer to find where the noise picked up by radios comes from. Jansky explored the skies and discovered radiation coming from the centre of our Milky Way, thereby starting the magnificent field of radioastronomy. A few years later, Bell asked another team, Arno Penzias and R. H. Wilson, to further study noise coming in from the outside and how best to deal with it. That resulted in the discovery of the big bang radiation. What could be more fundamental, yet more challenging? It came directly out of an applied engineering need.

A few years before that discovery, the physicists George Gamow, Ralph Alpher, and Robert Herman had predicted this background radiation. They predicted approximately the correct amount of radiation that would be out there, but thought it was too weak to detect. They reported their analysis in a paper few people read. Someone with the technical know-how would otherwise have realized that the predicted radiation was not too weak to detect. The theory had already been worked out, but the theorists, the experimentalists, and the engineers hadn't joined forces.

Finally, there's Zipf's law. George Kingsley Zipf started out asking about the frequency of the use of words in a given text, and found that if one word was used a thousand times, a hundred words would be used ten times, and a thousand words used just once in a given text. The number of times a word was used was inversely proportional to the number of such words. He then recognized that this also applies to wealth. If you have one family in Ontario worth $1 billion, there would be ten families worth $100 million, a hundred families worth $10 million, and so on. Although not exact, it turns out to be remarkably correct.

Zipf's law also applies to the size of storms. Their size depends inversely on the frequency of occurrence. What is peculiar about this is that it is closely related to what engineers and physicists know as "one over f noise," usually written as "1/f noise." In 1/f noise, the noise power is proportional to one over the frequency. One over f noise was a puzzle to theorists for a while because it doesn't make sense according to thermodynamics. Finally, theorists were able to account for it by recognizing complexity. One over f noise comes from the contribution of numerous variables acting together. Taking an example from human behaviour, intelligence, as measured by IQ, is normally distributed according to a bell-shaped curve. Most people have intelligence close to the average. You don't find many, or any, people with intelligence that is ten times the average. This is because intelligence is a single factor. But in human activities, there are levels of performance that differ by factors of 10 or 100 or 1000.

There are scientists who publish one hundred times the average number of scientific papers or who issue ten times the average number of patents, even though they may differ only a little in their IQs. This type of human productivity has been found to follow the same type of law. This is because it is not a single factor, such as intelligence, but innumerable factors that contribute to human activity. This leads to complexity where Zipf's law seems to apply. Each of these factors brings in its own bell-shaped curve, and the sum of the many bell-shaped curves results in a 1/f-type law.

What does Zipf's law or the 1/f law mean to scientific or technical productivity? There will always be an inherent uncertainty in planning and predicting scientific discovery and its influence on technology. Nonetheless, certain conditions must exist in order to ensure good productivity. Our understanding of the 1/f law says that each of many factors has to be favourable. Society must be interested in ideas and must value them; it must be excited by them and by new discoveries. We must accept a long-range approach. We must accept failures by encouraging trial and error, because no person can plan what scientific research is going to be successful. We must support people in a variety of situations, especially people with different ideas, because the different ideas are most likely to lead to something new. There must be a diversity of approach, a diversity of institutions, a diversity of people. There must also be a lot of interaction among them so they can exchange their thoughts.

The places where the activity is high, where many scientists are interacting, where there are outstanding people, where many factors are just right — those are the circumstances that are going to pay off the most. That doesn't mean we don't need the others, but we must see that there are places where the important factors all add up; that's where we can expect to find the most intensive productivity.

PART II

LIFE:
THE COSMIC
IMPERATIVE

MAX PERUTZ
Nobel Prize in Chemistry, 1962

*I*n *order to understand what functions proteins serve in the body and how they perform these functions, it is necessary to understand their structures. Not only does this help us comprehend protein action, but it may make it possible to design other proteins with useful properties.*

It wasn't until 1960, when Max Perutz and his colleague John C. Kendrew used a technique known as X-ray diffraction, that the first structure of complex protein molecules, specifically hemoglobin and myoglobin, were revealed. Perutz and Kendrew were awarded the Nobel Prize for chemistry for their "studies of the structures of globular proteins."

Originally from Vienna, Perutz has spent his entire scientific career in England where he began to study X-ray diffraction for analysing structures. While he was a graduate student at Cambridge in 1937, he started work on hemoglobin. Twenty-two years later, as director of the Unit for Molecular Biology in Cambridge, he finally solved its structure. Along the way, he developed techniques and approaches that have made it possible for others to solve protein structures.

The consequences of Perutz's work are extensive. His discoveries have led to a greater understanding of the relationship between structure and function of macromolecules in living systems. Today, together with site-directed mutogenesis (the work of another Nobel laureate, Michael Smith) and with advances in computing, the crystal structure of proteins is a starting point in understanding their mechanisms of action as well as in designing inhibitors and mimics.

Perutz has been honoured with the Royal and Copley medals of the Royal Society and with the Order of Merit by Her Majesty, Queen Elizabeth II. He continues to work at the Medical Research Council's Laboratory of Molecular Biology in Cambridge. He is concerned about the effects of science on society, which he discusses in the book Is Science Necessary?

Max Perutz

LIVING
MOLECULES

Oswald Avery, the man who dis-
covered what genes are made of, is one of my heroes. Born 130
years ago to poor English immigrants in Halifax, Nova Scotia,
Avery moved to New York at the age of ten when his father
became pastor of a Baptist church in one of the city's rundown
quarters. At first, Oswald wanted to become a minister like his
father, but after getting his bachelor's degree he changed his mind
and decided to become a doctor. He started his medical career
with a background in literature and philosophy rather than science, which was not necessary for entrance to medical school
then. On finding clinical practice unfulfilling, he turned to
research in bacteriology and, at the age of thirty-six, was
appointed bacteriologist at the Hospital of the Rockefeller Institute for Medical Research in New York, the best of its kind.

Until the late 1930s, pneumonia was a common, dreaded disease that killed about a third of those who contracted it,
including Avery's mother. In 1881 Louis Pasteur had discovered

that it was caused by a bacterium which he called pneumococcus. Avery wondered why some of the patients in the pneumonia ward of his hospital died, while others recovered, even though they were all infected by the same bacteria.

The first step on the road to unravelling the mystery was made by his collaborator, A. Raymond Dochez, who found that the blood in the urine of the moribund patients contained an unusual soluble substance that was not present in the blood or the urine of recovered patients. Dochez and Avery isolated the substance but, not being chemists, misidentified it as a protein. It wasn't until many years later when they were joined by the chemist Michael Heidelburger that he identified it as a polysaccharide, a molecule made of chains of sugar-like molecules.

The significance of this discovery became clear only in 1922 when Fred Griffith, a bacteriologist at the laboratory of the Ministry of Health in London found that there are two types of pneumococci: non-virulent ones that appear to be small and naked, which Griffith called rough, and bigger, virulent ones covered in a slimy mucous shell, which he called smooth. This slimy shell was made of the same sugary substance that Dochez and Avery had found in the blood of the urine of the infected patients.

Avery tried making a vaccine of the sugar-coating, but it did not work. Progress was stalled until 1928, when Griffith tried an experiment that any sane person would have told him was useless and crazy. He infected mice with a mixture of live, rough (non-virulent) bacteria and dead, smooth (virulent) ones that he had killed by boiling. A few days later, the mice were dead and full of virulent smooth bacteria. The dead, smooth bacteria had transformed the live, rough bacteria into smooth ones. They had induced a heritable change in the rough bacteria, an extraordinary, inexplicable, and unbelievable finding. In fact, very few believed it, and Avery took no notice of Griffith's result until one of his collaborators confirmed it when Avery was ill in bed. He then did away with the mice by incubating a mixture of live, rough and dead, smooth pneumococci in broth and getting the same transformation.

Avery became determined to find out what caused this result. He was convinced that it must be a single substance, but since a bacterium contains thousands of different proteins and other substances, the search for a single one seemed hopeless. One obvious candidate was the mucous shell itself, but this was quickly ruled out because it was inactive. Avery and his colleagues searched in vain for about twelve years until Avery's collaborator, Melvyn McCarty, discovered a way to break open the bacterial coat with bile juice and dissolve the bacterial contents in water. When he and Avery added some of this solution to a culture of rough bacteria, they were transformed into smooth, virulent bacteria.

At first Avery and McCarty thought that a protein might be the transforming substance. To test this idea, they treated the bacterial extract with enzymes known to split proteins which John Howard Northrop and Roger Herriott, two biochemists at the Rockefeller Institute, had just isolated, but the enzymes left the transforming activity intact.

Next they wondered about ribonucleic acid. They were fortunate because Moses Kunitz, another biochemist at the Rockefeller Institute, had just isolated the first enzyme known to split it. He gave them some of his enzyme, but it also left the transforming activity intact. Wondering what else there might be, they added alcohol to their solution, which precipitated a white, slimy gel. They dissolved this gel in water and added it to their culture of rough pneumococi. The next morning, they found that it had transformed them into smooth ones. What was the gel made of? Staining with analytical dyes showed that it was made of deoxyribonucleic acid, DNA. As little as a million millionth of a gram proved to be sufficient to induce the transformation. To make sure that the activity was not due to contaminating protein or ribonucleic acid, they treated their solution of DNA with the same enzymes that were known to split these substances, but they did not touch the activity.

As a final test, Avery and his colleagues decided to treat their solution with an enzyme that splits DNA. They had to work for months to isolate such an enzyme from animal intestines and to purify it. When it was finally ready for the trial, it destroyed the transforming activity of their extract. It was the final proof that the transforming activity rested in the DNA. Since the transformation was heritable, the DNA had to contain a gene: an unbelievable result in 1943 when DNA was universally believed to be no more than an inert skeleton supporting the proteins.

The result was so revolutionary that Avery himself was reluctant to accept it and write it up for publication. The paper by him, Colin M. MacLeod, and Melvyn McCarty finally appeared in the *Journal of Experimental Medicine* in 1944. Its wording was cautious in the extreme and it did not even mention the word *gene*, but careful reading shows the evidence to have been absolutely conclusive. Historians wondered whether Avery himself was aware of having isolated a gene, until Robert Olby unearthed a letter from a visitor to the Rockefeller Institute, the Australian biologist Macfarlane Burnett, to his wife, telling her that Avery had isolated a gene.

Avery was a meticulous, retiring bachelor who lived for his research. He took out no patents, wrote no books, and never went on lecture tours. He made his great discovery, one of the most important of this century, when he was about to retire. He should have received the Nobel Prize, but most biochemists, including those on the Nobel Committee, were reluctant to believe that DNA has such an important function. Only the Royal Society of London conferred on him their highest honour, the Copley Medal. Fred Griffith, who might have shared the Nobel Prize with Avery, had they both lived, was killed by a German bomb during the London Blitz in 1940.

DNA is made of long chains in which phosphates alternate with sugar-like rings of deoxyribose. Attached to each sugar is a base made of rings of carbon and nitrogen. The bases are of four different kinds called adenine, thymine, guanine, and cytosine, or A, T, G, and C for short. It seemed a dull, monotonous molecule; that was why nobody thought it had an important function.

On Linus Pauling's principle that in a long chain molecule,

chemically equivalent or near equivalent units should occupy equivalent positions, which is possible only in a helix, Francis Crick argued that DNA should have a helical structure. X-ray diffraction pictures taken by Maurice Wilkins and Rosalind Franklin at King's College, London, seemed to confirm this belief. Their X-ray pictures suggested that fibres of DNA contain either two or three chains wound around each other, but James Watson argued on genetic grounds that two were more likely. Do they run in the same or opposite directions? One of Franklin's X-ray pictures suggested that the structure possessed a symmetry consistent only with anti-parallel chains.

This information was useful, but would have been insufficient to build an atomic model of DNA had it not been for two of those lucky coincidences that can turn failure into success.

Our colleague John Kendrew happened to be friendly with Erwin Chargaff, the Hungarian-born biochemist at Columbia University who was working on the chemistry of DNA. One day Chargaff visited Cambridge, and Kendrew invited him to dinner in his college together with Watson and Crick. There, Chargaff drew their attention to a paper he had recently published in an obscure Swiss journal, *Experientia,* showing that in the DNA from several different sources the ratios of A to T and G to C were always near unity.

It was a vital clue. If DNA was made of two helices, Chargaff's result suggested that A in one chain is linked to a T in its opposite chain, and G in one chain is always linked to T in its opposite chain. But how? The chemical formulae of the bases suggested hydrogen bonds, but an ambiguity left the nature of the bonds uncertain. By another unbelievable piece of good luck, Watson and Crick shared their office with Gerry Donohue, a young chemist from Linus Pauling's laboratory at the California Institute of Technology, who happened to know the answer. There was no ambiguity: one set of formulae was right and the other was wrong. Armed with that information, Watson was able to predict the correct hydrogen bonds between the bases (except that he left one bond out).

Watson and Crick's model can be thought of as a spiral staircase with the base pairs as the steps and the phosphate-sugar chain as the banisters. The model suggested that the four different bases form the genetic alphabet and that the genetic information is laid down in form of their sequence along the chain. Moreover, the model implied a simple mechanism whereby this information might be copied each time a cell divides. Suppose the double helix untwists and the two chains separate from each other. Since the sequence of bases along the chain must be complementary, G always paired with C and A with T, each chain could become a template for the synthesis of a new complementary chain. In this way, one parent double helix could give birth to two daughter double helices, each with the same sequence of bases as the parent.

DNA carries an enormous amount of information. The minute head of a human sperm contains a metre of DNA. This length of DNA carries 3,000 million bases. If these were letters of the alphabet, they would be equivalent to a library of 5,000 volumes. This is the amount of information needed to make us what we are. Each time a cell divides, this information is copied with, on the average, only a single misprint. This is one of the great wonders of nature. No human printer could do this.

What does DNA do? Its sole function is to code for the sequence of the different kinds of amino acids in proteins. All chemical reactions in living cells are catalyzed, or speeded up, by enzymes, and all enzymes are proteins. The oxygen we breathe is reduced to water by enzymes; the food we eat is broken down and turned into chemical energy by enzymes; and enzymes in our muscles convert chemical energy into mechanical energy. A special enzyme is used for every one of the thousands of different chemical reactions that make up life. Enzymes are fantastically efficient. For example, hydrogen peroxide is quite stable in water at room temperature, but one molecule of the enzyme catalase breaks it down into water and oxygen at the rate of half a million molecules per second. Enzymes can catalyze reactions at body temperature and near neutral pH, for which a chemist would need powerful solvents, high temperatures, or strong acids or bases.

Proteins consist of chains of exactly twenty different kinds of amino acids. Once a chain with a specific sequence has been synthesized in the cell, it folds up spontaneously to an exactly determined shape, often to a more or less round molecule of precise structure that is needed for its specific catalytic activity. So the enzyme that splits hydrogen peroxide looks quite different from one that splits sugar.

I spent most of my working life trying to find out what hemoglobin, the protein of the red blood cells, looks like and how it works. Hemoglobin carries oxygen from the lungs to the tissues and facilitates the return transport of carbon dioxide from the tissues back to the lungs. It is a two-way respiratory carrier. It consists of four chains, one pair with 141 and the other with 146 amino acids, and four red pigment groups called hemes, each carrying an atom of iron at its centre. The chains are coiled into helices, and the helices folded to make a roughly spherical molecule, with its four hemes in separate pockets on its surface.

Each of the four iron atoms is capable of combining with one oxygen molecule in the lungs and releasing it in the tissues. Early in the century, the Danish physiologist Christian Bohr discovered that the four heme irons do not react with oxygen independently, but that they interact so the avidity for oxygen rises with the amount of oxygen taken up. Conversely, the liberation of oxygen is eased with the amount of oxygen already liberated. So the behaviour of hemoglobin follows the biblical parallel of the rich and the poor: "To him who hath shall be given." This makes oxygen transport very efficient, because it ensures that a small increase in the partial pressure of oxygen leads to a huge uptake, and a small decrease to a large release of oxygen.

Physiologists used to attribute this behaviour to interaction between the four hemes, but I found it to be due to a change of structure undergone by the entire hemoglobin molecule every time oxygen is taken up and released. In this way, hemoglobin alternates between a purple structure with low oxygen affinity which dominates in the veins, and a scarlet one with high affinity which dominates in the arteries. So hemoglobin is a moving mechanism, not an oxygen tank but a breathing molecule.

This was a thrilling discovery, but is it any use? Has it cured anybody yet? For many years I doubted that my life's work on the structure and the mechanism of this molecule could benefit medicine, but recently my colleague Kiyoshi Nagai has used the structure and the methods pioneered by Dr. Michael Smith to engineer a genetically modified hemoglobin that can be used as a substitute for transfused blood. This is now in phase 2 clinical trial and, so far, the results look hopeful.

Protein engineering has already brought many other benefits to medicine, among them the first successful attempt at somatic gene therapy on one of the gravest inherited diseases. Babies born with an inherited deficiency of the enzyme adenosine deaminase lack an immune system. Being defenseless against infections, they can be raised only in sterile tents or rooms, cut off from playmates and people. French Anderson and his colleagues in the United States have introduced the lacking gene into two baby girls by removing a little of their bone marrow, infecting and incubating it with a virus that carries the lacking gene but can no longer replicate, and reintroducing this marrow into the babies' bones. After injections spread over two years, synthesis of the missing enzyme is well established and the girls can live normal lives, go to school, play with other children, and even ice skate. By now, more than two hundred trials of somatic gene therapy are in progress in the United States. Adenosine deaminase is a rare disease that Anderson chose as a target for a first attempt because, among other things, it is such a hopeless one. Most of the trials are directed at cystic fibrosis, one of the most frequent diseases among Europeans. Great benefits may also result from the combination of DNA technology and immunology, because this may lead to new cancer therapies and may open the way to the first effective treatments of autoimmune diseases such as rheumatoid arthritis and disseminated sclerosis.

Recombinant DNA technology promises a great future for those willing to grasp it. To those who watch the signs of the times, it seems plain that the twenty-first century will see scientific revolutions as great as those of the seventeenth century. But who can tell through what trials and contests the civilized world will have to pass in the course of this new reformation.

But I verily believe that, come what will, the part which Canada may play in the battle is a grand and noble one. She may prove to the world that for one people, at any rate, despotism and demagogy are not the necessary alternatives of government; that freedom and order are not incompatible; that reverence is the handmaid of knowledge; that free discussion is the life of truth and of true unity in a nation.

Will Canada play this part? This depends upon how you, the public, deal with science. Cherish her, venerate her, follow her message faithfully and implicitly in their application to all branches of human thought and the future of this people will be greater than in the past.

Listen to those who would silence and crush her and I fear our children will see the glory of Canada vanishing like Arthur in the mist.

These are the final paragraphs of a lecture given by the great naturalist T. H. Huxley in London 135 years ago. I merely substituted Canada for England.

JAMES DEWEY WATSON

Nobel Prize in Physiology or Medicine, 1962

*U*nderstanding the structure of a mole-
cule can give clues about its function. This concept is central to the field of
molecular biology, a field that saw its great advancement with the discov-
ery of the structure of DNA (deoxyribonucleic acid).

The DNA molecule has the shape of a double helix, a simple structure
resembling a gently twisting ladder. The rails of the ladder are made of
alternating units of phosphate and the sugar deoxyribose. The rungs are
composed of a pair of nitrogen-containing nucleotides. James D. Watson
shared the 1962 Nobel Prize in physiology or medicine with Francis
Crick and Maurice Wilkins for their discovery of DNA.

Each nucleotide within a rung of the DNA ladder is always paired
with the same complementary nucleotide. This means that one-half of the
molecule can serve as a template for the construction of the other half.
During cell division, the DNA helix unzips and two new molecules are
formed from the half-ladder templates, explaining how identical copies of
parental DNA can be passed on to two daughter cells.

A native of Chicago, Watson received his B.S. from the University of Chicago and a Ph.D. from Indiana University, both in zoology. He joined the faculty at Harvard University in 1955, resigning in 1976 to become full-time director of Cold Spring Harbor Laboratory, a position he has held since 1968. Under his direction, the financially strapped laboratory was revitalized. Watson steered research into the field of tumour virology, leading to an understanding of cancer genes (oncogenes) and the molecular basis of cancer. In addition to cancer research, plant molecular biology, cell biochemistry, and neuroscience, the laboratory functions as a postgraduate university for DNA science. He is currently the laboratory's president.

Watson also held the post of director of the National Center for Human Genome Research, a position he left after launching a worldwide effort to map and sequence the human genome in 1992.

Watson has been honoured with the John J. Carty Gold Medal of the National Academy of Sciences and the Copley Award of the Royal Society.

James Dewey Watson

THE HUMAN
GENOME PROJECT

*A*fter Francis Crick and I had found the double helix, we realized that the genetic information was stored in a digital-like way on linear information-bearing molecules with four letters. To go from that information to the confirmation of what we suspected the genes did — provide the information to make proteins — took roughly fifteen years, to 1968. When that was done, we were both happy and stuck, not knowing how next to proceed. Though in the genetic code we had the Rosetta Stone that let us translate between the languages of the genes and the structure of proteins, we couldn't look at individual DNA molecules and so we couldn't look at individual genes. Thus our field remained, for the most part, impractical. We never thought about making money, and our enemies at that time often were the deans at the university. They seemed to pay more attention and higher salaries to the organic chemists who also generated wealth than to people who only generated ideas.

This picture suddenly changed in 1973 with the arrival of recombinant DNA and the potential it gave for cloning genes (isolating and identifying individual pieces of DNA). Once we began to have genes, we could work out their structure and know the amino acid sequences of their protein products. Vast new areas of science quickly opened up, among which was human genetics, a field that had been almost closed before.

Ordinary genetics is done by breeding drosophila and examining the offspring. Such genetic crosses obviously cannot be done with human beings, and though we could hypothesize, we often could not be certain whether a gene was dominant or recessive or where on one of the twenty-four different chromosomes it lay. We were lucky if it was on the X chromosome because of sex-linked inheritance. That at least told us it was on a definite chromosome. But then, within a decade of the discovery of recombinant DNA, we didn't have to breed people to study their genetics.

The key insight that set human genetics moving was the realization that cloned DNA sequence differences — polymorphisms — were splendid genetic markers that could be accurately followed in multigenerational families. Using these polymorphisms, a high resolution human genetic map could be made. With the map in hand, you could see whether a genetic trait co-segregated with one of the large series of DNA markers that had been assigned to precise chromosomal locations. You didn't look to see whether a person had blue eyes; you looked to see what pieces of DNA a particular trait accompanied.

By 1984 we began assigning the first genetic disease genes to autosomes (not the sex chromosomes). Huntington's disease was first found on chromosome four, and soon after, cystic fibrosis was located on chromosome seven. Already by then we realized that human genetics would go much faster if we set up an internationally organized effort that became known as the Human Genome Project. Using it we could build an infrastructure for genetic mapping and, eventually, gene cloning. Though gene cloning was possible without the Human Genome Project, it usually required a heroic effort at individual research sites, such as the one mounted at the University of Toronto. Moreover, successful cloning was likely to be limited to cleanly defined genetic diseases occurring frequently enough to be able to map easily. If we went to look for the genes for a rare disease or where its inheritance was murky, we didn't have the tools.

The proposal to start the Human Genome Project to work out the complete DNA sequence of the human genome was first made in 1984, and came to a head in 1986. The scientific community as a whole was initially opposed to this proposal for two reasons: it would cost money, taking financing away from other academics; and it didn't appear to require clever participants. The notion of making a very high resolution map didn't sound like an inspired idea. Almost without exception, the better younger scientists working on DNA were against spending masses of money on totally sequencing the DNA of even the smallest bacteria.

Fortunately, besides young people, there are old people. Perhaps because we feel closer to disease than the young ones, we really wanted to find the genes for Alzheimer's, for example. Essentially it was the old person establishment that endorsed the project, and since Congress is largely made up of elderly people, they listened to us. I later ran the project, since I'd helped to get it started, with the hope that we would attain a much faster understanding of human beings. I also hoped to sneak in a few other projects, such as working out the complete genetic structure of some bacteria — E. coli, drosophila, C. elegans, and yeast. These sorts of objectives had intrigued me as a biologist. For example, by getting both the European community and the National Institutes of Health into the act, we are going to find out the complete structure of the yeast Saccharomyces Cerevisiae chromosomes by 1996.

The main objective of the program today, however, remains to work out the sequence of bases along all twenty-four human chromosomes. You can think of each base in DNA as a letter in a very long word (gene) in an immense book whose three billion letters code for some 100,000 genes. This large size is the reason so many people were against this project at the start. Only ten years ago it cost about $20 a base pair, for a possible total of $60 billion for the project. But good scientists are always optimistic, and some of us believed as early as 1987 that the human sequence could be done for $3 billion if the project was run correctly.

The project was to be carried out in several phases. First, we had to make a very high resolution genetic map in order to place disease genes as close as possible along the chromosomes. Secondly, we had to isolate and order the DNA pieces that encompassed all the genes. And thirdly we had to sequence those pieces of DNA. Today, thanks to work being done in a number of places around the world, particularly in Paris at Genethon with Jean Weissenbach, we have the high resolution genetic map needed. Even better, we can now automate the mapping procedure, and more and more diseases can be rapidly mapped to precise chromosome sites. The ordered arranging of pieces of human DNA from one end of the chromosome to the other is a more difficult objective. But we have already done it for the smallest chromosome, 21, as well as for the Y chromosome and much of the X chromosome. At this moment, however, there only exist imperfect physical maps for the remaining chromosomes. But even so, researchers now working on a particular disease can usually get DNA from their respective chromosomal region without having to isolate it themselves.

The next step will be to sequence the DNA, which is more complicated in human DNA than in bacteria because human DNA is split into functional and non-functional regions. Happily, there are a lot of good tricks for sequencing, and, in fact, human DNA sequencing can now be done at the mega (10^6) base level. The resulting large number of letters to scan for their gene components is beyond the eye to interpret. These days you can only make sense of the sequence by using a computer. Fortunately, computers still get better every year, so the computing aspect isn't the limiting factor. The costs are still largely in preparing the DNA for sequencing. However, it's hard to get the precise cost of sequencing because scientists keep telling you that they're doing a trial run. But you do know how much money you're putting in and how many bases are being sequenced per year. These days the cost seems to be about $1 a base pair, and we will probably get the price down to 50 cents a base pair (I'd be happier with 25 cents). All of this is being done by automation that uses the basic 1975 sequencing procedure of Fred Sanger. Since then there have been only two great advances beyond Sanger's. In 1984 came the first polymerase chain reaction of Kary Mullis. Without it, we would have needed to spend much more money than we now have for the genome project. The second main advance was the development at CalTech and the European Molecular Biology Laboratory of automated machines for DNA sequencing. Using these machines, there are now a number of very good sequencing centres. Already several of them can sequence more than 10 million base pairs a year.

As we get more and more human DNA sequences, we will increasingly be able to tell if a person is predisposed to various traits. While this information will be very useful in understanding and diagnosing diseases, it can also present a number of ethical and moral problems. So when we set up the genome project at NIH, we decided to spend 3 percent of our money on ethics. The number was not based on any concrete principles, but 2 percent seemed too little and 10 percent too much. It's gone up to 5 percent now. But merely spending money talking or writing about the ethical problems will not necessarily help us in resolving them.

The insurance of individual genetic privacy, for example, cannot be handled simply by passing legislation. If someone tests positively for a disease, who are they obliged to tell? People may not want their employer or insurance company to know, but should the spouse and the children know? If you are an identical twin and your genetic makeup is identical to your sibling's, should you share knowledge that you've learned about yourself with your twin? There are bureaucratic dimensions, too. When testing is done, one would want to know that the testing was done properly. But the result is bound to be an increase in the cost of the tests because government agencies such as the FDA would get involved. And then there's the question of affordability. If the test is too expensive, will your health insurance pay for it? And what of education? Almost from the start we knew our 3 percent wasn't going to make a dent in the fact that most Americans haven't heard of Gregor Mendel, the Austrian scientist who formulated the laws of heredity. When talk turns to dominant and recessive genes, people turn off. But if they aren't educated, how will they make informed decisions about the genetic tests that will increasingly give parents the ability to have children unencumbered by genetic disease?

For many people, however, this growing ability to influence the genetic makeup of our children is a mixed blessing that will inevitably lead to a revival of eugenic-like thinking. Eugenics, or the improvement of the human species by the careful selection of parents, started with Charles Darwin's cousin, Francis Galton. Galton was an exponent of Social Darwinism, the theory of survival of the fittest applied to humans. This was very convenient for people like Galton, because they inherited wealth and liked to assume that people who had the wealth also had better genes. Social Darwinism at first was just talk — the only way to have applied it in practice was to marry into a good family and have lots of children. Then Mendel's laws were rediscovered in 1900, and with the basis of heredity known, scientists began to wonder what could be done about human beings. They knew they couldn't breed them, but they could follow how supposedly good and bad traits passed from one generation to another.

The Cold Spring Harbor Laboratory on Long Island, New York, with which I've now been associated for more than twenty-five years, began breeding a variety of plants and animals immediately after the rediscovery of Mendel's laws. Charles Davenport thought, however, that since human beings were more important than sheep, domestic animals, and plants, Cold Spring Harbor should also initiate a genetic program on humans. A way to do this came with the help of a wealthy woman, Mrs. Marie Harriman, whose daughter had been a summer student at

Cold Spring Harbor. It was she who gave money to set up a eugenics record station to collect pedigrees showing how genetic diseases are inherited within extended multigenerational families.

At the Eugenics Record Station, an attractive building that reflected wealth, a yearly summer course was given how to take pedigrees. Its students were largely girls from good families who came to learn basic principles of Mendelian genetics. They learned about diseases such as albinism, a recessive disease that would occur in some of the offspring of a pair of heterozygotes, as well as traits like cataracts that appeared to be due to dominant genes. Their concern, however, went beyond simple diseases and human traits, such as "wanderlust, alcoholic, feeble-minded, sex-offender, gambler, and thief" — traits they naively believed to have large hereditary components. One family was even described as "showing good hereditary, contaminated by slight alcoholic hereditary and town life."

Unable to understand why individuals would behave in unacceptable ways, certain eugenicists argued, for example, that one must be feeble-minded to be a prostitute. However, there was then virtually no evidence that any of the personality or moral traits that they found so undesirable were hereditary. Consequently, many dreadful miscarriages of justice occurred when some 40,000 women were sterilized in the 1920s-40s for supposed feeble-mindedness or mental disease.

We should realize, however, that at this time there were no effective treatments for any mental illness, be it schizophrenia, manic-depressive disease, acute depression, or anxiety. Vast mental hospitals had sprung up all over the United States and Europe, and the entrance into their often "snake pit"-like atmosphere was frequently an irreversible event. So the unmitigated horrors of mental disease had to loom even larger in the public mind than they do today with drug treatments, admittedly some far from perfect, now available for most forms of serious mental disease. But back in the 1920s and 30s, the diagnosis of serious mental disease was essentially a lifelong death sentence. The then existing eugenics world did not believe itself evil for advocating sterilization.

They saw the potential for preventing future personal tragedies as being worth the price of a few mistakes resulting from their incomplete scientific knowledge. The missionary-type zeal of the American eugenicists, however, increasingly worried many of the better American geneticists, and by the 1930s warnings were voiced that the science behind the sterilization programs was virtually nonexistent.

No authoritative questioning existed in Germany, however, where the eugenics movement was already strongly endorsed by the Nazi followers, even before they assumed power in 1933. They then immediately promoted a massive sterilization program involving virtually all of the long-term patients in German psychiatric hospitals. This German effort soon had objectives beyond the supposed elimination from the Aryan peoples of genes leading to mental disease. In 1937, compulsory sterilization was extended to some 25,000 "coloured" people, resulting from "mixed" cohabitation in Southwest Africa. Even worse, soon after World War II started, the already sterilized psychiatric population was sent to the gas chambers, which soon after were employed equally grotesquely to eliminate the supposedly genetically inferior Jewish, gypsy, and Slav populations. When the existence of these genocide programs came to light after the war ended, the German academic genetic and anthropology communities that had so strongly backed eugenics stood exposed, and their shame extended to all eugenic movements independent of their past relations with their German compatriots.

So it is not surprising that the term eugenics still conveys such negative connotations today and that strong apprehension exists among many people as to whether governments should play any role in determining the genetic destinies of their citizens. On the other hand, many genetic diseases continue to create wretched human tragedies, both for their immediate victims and those who love and take care of them. No family wants to be a victim of one of those diseases, and many, if not the majority of our citizens, have welcomed the arrival of real human genetics and the subsequent disease gene isolations that provide knowledge about underlying molecular defects as well as possible genetic diagnoses at the DNA level.

Obviously we would like to find cures for all serious genetic diseases either through the development of drugs that counteract their respective molecular defects or through gene therapy procedures which introduce into the diseased cells the good copies of their respective diseased genes. We have no reason, however, to express confidence that gene therapy procedures will work for most genetic diseases nor should we count on the development of miracle-type drugs that, let's say, can cure the severe mental retardation caused by the fragile X gene. The only certain way to prevent the agony of most serious genetic diseases is to use abortion when prenatal genetic diagnosis reveals that a fetus, if allowed to come to term, will be severely genetically impaired. This procedure is already used when the presence of an extra chromosome 21 reveals that a fetus will develop into a Down's syndrome child. Most prospective parents when presented with this genetic diagnosis elect to abort, and in those population groups where Down's screening is widespread, Down's incidence is significantly falling. But there also exist many peoples who avoid such screening believing that all life is sacred and no future genetic defect warrants what they consider the murder of a human being.

However, even among those ethical and religious groups who consider abortion the appropriate response to the threat of a seriously debilitating genetic disease, there now exist many individuals strongly opposed to abortion used to control nonlife-threatening treats, such as sex, eye colour, or stature. But the question has to be asked: Who will be harmed by such decisions? In contrast, once we let the state have any say in affecting the genetic makeup of our children, we are bound to be restricted by decisions that must seem arbitrarily harmful to many people in the multicultural societies most of us now inhabit. We would have to expect that any laws passed or regulations put forth would seriously restrict the freedom of many families to choose what they believe to be good for them. How, say, should prospective parents feel if told that they could abort a potential Down's child but not one pre-destined to have only partially curable, severe dyslexia. And while we can be sure that many individuals would seriously oppose abortion used to prevent the birth of homosexual children, there are bound to be other parts of society that would welcome genetic procedures used for the compulsory abortion of poten-tially homosexual individuals.

I therefore believe we would soon regret allowing any govern-ment, no matter how initially well-intentioned, to have any control over the genetic makeup of its citizens. For better or worse, only the prospective mother (working with the father when he is likely to help in the support of their children) should be involved in the decision as to whether or not to use genetic tests to help them have the children they desire. Of course, I know that long into the foreseeable future many individuals will continue to question this newfound right to supposedly play God. But I feel strongly that this is the wrong question to ask. More important is the question as to whether or not we will be failing in our responsibilities as human beings if we do not use genetics to help parents bear children unencumbered by the consequences of a bad throw of the genetic dice.

MICHAEL SMITH

Nobel Prize in Chemistry, 1993

*G*enerally recognized as "the father of site-directed mutagenesis," Michael Smith developed the technique that has given rise to a new field of protein engineering. Site-directed mutagenesis allows gene sequences to be changed in a specific manner in specific regions of DNA by using synthetic oligonucleotides, short, synthetic DNA fragments. It also allows researchers to examine the role of specific amino acids.

Smith's method established a new approach to studying the relationship between the structure and the function of proteins. By mutating a gene, it became possible to change any amino acid in a protein to see what role it plays in its biological activity. It allowed a better understanding of how biological systems function. The method can be used to improve enzymes, make them more stable, or even engineer new proteins with specific properties and functions. Smith shared the 1993 Nobel Prize in Chemistry with Kary Mullis, who invented the polymerase chain reaction (PCR) method for amplifying DNA in vitro.

Born in Blackpool, England, in 1932, Smith was not able to attend Oxford or Cambridge because of his lack of proficiency in Latin. He obtained his education from the University of Manchester and came to Vancouver in 1956 for postdoctoral studies. He worked for the Fisheries Research Board of Canada laboratory before joining the University of British Columbia faculty in Vancouver in 1966. Smith established the Biotechnology Laboratory at the University of British Columbia in 1987, an interdisciplinary institute where he is director. As well as heading the Network of Centres of Excellence on Protein Engineering, he has been a career investigator with the Medical Research Council of Canada since 1966.

An avid outdoorsman, Smith enjoys the rugged beauty of British Columbia.

Michael Smith

SYNTHETIC DNA AND BIOLOGY

*T*he idea that chemistry can contribute to an understanding of biology is not new. Jacob Berzelius, a scientist of the early 1800s, is the man who invented the system by which the elements' names are abbreviated (H for hydrogen, He for helium, Na for sodium, and so on). In a letter to the king of Sweden in 1806 he said, "Of all the sciences that will contribute most to the understanding of biology, it is chemistry." Of course, he was a chemist, so one might expect him to say that. Perhaps he was lobbying for grants. Nonetheless, it was a bold, if vague, prediction.

A much more specific prediction was made by Emil Fischer, the second person to win a Nobel Prize for chemistry. In 1917 he said that chemistry would do something for genetics, which was extremely daring and forward looking of him considering that the critical events which made that possible did not occur until 1944 when Oswald Avery, Melvyn McCarty, and Colin

McLeod discovered that DNA was responsible for inheritance. Erwin Chargaff, in his studies on DNA chemistry, came up with the unusual and unexpected finding that the amount of adenine, thymine, or guanine and cytosine were always the same in different DNAs, although the general composition changed from species to species. Using this information and that from Rosalind Franklin's fibre diffraction studies, Jim Watson and Francis Crick came up with the double helix in 1953.

As a young chemist in 1956, I decided to come to North America. By pure good luck, I ended up in the laboratory of Gobind Khorana at the University of British Columbia who, with Marshall Nirenberg, elucidated the genetic code. That explained the relationship between the sequences of base pairs in DNA and the sequence of amino acids in proteins. Khorana discovered the synthetic DNA methodology, and from that went on to elucidate the genetic code for which he, Marshall Nirenberg, and Robert Holly won the Nobel Prize for physiology or medicine in 1968.

An interesting story lies behind Khorana's presence at the University of British Columbia. Gordon Shrum, head of the British Columbia Research Council, an applied research institute at UBC, was also on the board of the National Research Council. Dr. Shrum decided that British Columbia needed to do more basic research, so he approached Dr. Edward Steacie, NRC's president, for funding. Steacie gave Shrum $25,000 to set up a basic research program at what otherwise was an applied research institute.

Shrum went to England to interview many people, including Dr. Alexander Todd (now Lord Todd) of Cambridge University. Todd pointed out that there was a young East Indian in his laboratory for whom there were no job prospects in India (or in England in the 1950s). As a consequence, Shrum offered Khorana a job. Khorana accepted, and went to the library to look up where British Columbia and Vancouver were in the atlas.

He arrived there in 1952, and the department heads in this applied institute had a meeting chaired by Dr. Shrum where they discussed what things Dr. Khorana should work on that might be useful. After listening to their discussion for a while, Dr. Shrum said, "Gentlemen, we didn't hire a man of Dr. Khorana's talents to tell him what to do."

Khorana's contributions were based on an accidental discovery. He was trying to develop a method to degrade DNA sequentially but instead did a reaction that polymerized DNA. He realized he had tapped into something of significance, and used it for three cardinal purposes: to study the mechanization of action of DNA and RNA metabolizing enzymes; to elucidate the genetic code using synthetic oligonucleotides, short DNA fragments of defined sequence; and, together with enzymes as synthetic tools, to synthesize the first DNA gene. In synthesizing a gene, he developed most of the basic synthetic technology which is the foundation of modern molecular genetics and its progeny — genetic engineering and the biotechnology industry.

A lot of discoveries contributed to this technology of genetic engineering: the isolation of small, manageable chromosomes; the isolation of enzymes that cut DNA into specific fragments; the isolation of enzymes that join those fragments together precisely so they are biologically viable; the discovery of methodologies for putting DNA from a test tube into a living cell, having it stay in that living cell, and replicate and function in succeeding generations of cells derived from that living cell; rapid methods of DNA sequence determination; and improvements in the chemical synthesis of DNA beyond the methodologies developed by Khorana. A variety of well-known people contributed to these discoveries. These discoveries were made, not for an applied objective, but because these people were interested in biology and wanted to find out about the biochemistry and the enzymology of genetics. What resulted was something that could be used.

Let me explain what this technology allows us to do. Bacteria have one large chromosome, but also some smaller mini-chromosomes called plasmids which just encode a few genes. An animal cell has many chromosomes with a lot of DNA in them. We can use an enzyme to cut the small plasmids just once and the larger DNA into many fragments; in the case of a bacterial cell, it might be a thousand fragments; in the case of a yeast cell, a few thousand fragments. In the case of a human cell, it would be a million or so fragments. If we mix those fragments together with a large amount of the small chromosome pieces (relative to the other pieces) and add the joining enzyme, we can make recombinant DNA. (Joining the DNA from any source with that of another source forms hybrid DNA genes.) By choosing the ratios correctively, just one of those fragments of the human cell will be incorporated in the recombinant circle.

If we take that DNA in solution at high dilution and add it to a bacterial cell that does not contain any mini-chromosomes, some of those bacterial cells will take up one copy of that mini-chromosome and they will be propagated there — with just one piece of DNA out of those million that came out of the human cell. There will be a million different bacterial cells, each one with a different piece of recombinant DNA in it. If that suspension of cells is diluted and plated out on a nutrient plate, we get droplets, each of which has one bacterial cell which will form a colony containing just one piece of human DNA. A million different colonies will be distributed in what is called a genetic library, a strange library in which there are no labels on the books. One of the problems molecular biologists face is that they would like to know, say, where gene A is: which of the million fragments has gene A.

Adenine bonds with thymine, and guanine bonds with cytosine, and that produces the double helix. The bonds are so-called hydrogen bonds, which are somewhat weaker than ordinary chemical bonds. There are three important things about that double helix. First, the way it allows DNA to replicate because the two strands can be pulled apart and each strand can act as a template to produce another copy of the strand that was removed; once separated and by using an appropriate enzyme, one double strand can become two double strands and two can go to four, and so on. Second, the chemistry of a living cell, the chemistry of the environment, and the radiation of the environment can damage DNA. They can, for instance, cause an adenine to fall off, or they can cause a cytosine to lose an amine to become uracil. Over the course of evolution, the living cell has developed scanning proteins, which are constantly looking over the DNA for damage. The enzymes can identify that damage. They will clip a bit of DNA out of that one strand around that damage and then, using the undamaged template, use a synthetic mechanism to correct the damage. That's happening all the time.

To give you some physical feeling of how significant this process is, think about yourself. Each of you inherited one metre of DNA from your mother and one metre of DNA from your father. That fertilized egg cell with two metres of DNA replicated and replicated, and now each of you is an assemblage of between 10 and 100 million million cells, which means each of you contains between 20,000 and 200,000 million kilometres of DNA generated by replication of those two metres you inherited from your parents. As adults, most of the cells are not replicating, except for the cells in bone marrow replicating to produce more red cells, and cells in intestines, which are sloughed off and replaced constantly. So there are new cells and new DNA being formed. Each of you, in the last sixty seconds, synthesized 100,000 kilometres of DNA because of that replication process. Not many of you felt it. Again, I mention the damage that is occurring. Each cell throughout your body has about 10,000 damaging events occur within it every day, damaging DNA by depurinating, de-aminating, and so forth, and synthesis is occurring. So again in the last sixty seconds, each of us synthesized about 20,000 kilometres of DNA just repairing the damage that occurs all the time in the cells. If reparation of the damage in living cells wasn't happening, all of us would have been dead with cancer a long time ago.

The third reason the double helix is important is because chemists can work with one, or with a bit of one, of those strands in a test tube. In about 1968, we wanted to know if a short synthetic piece of DNA of defined sequence could be used as a tool to recognize a naturally occurring piece of nucleic acid. There was some knowledge; Peter Gilham had done preliminary work with random-length, chemically synthesized fragments and had found that Watson-Crick structures formed and that they were stable. One question we had to ask, though, was how long an oligonucleotide would have to be to recognize a unique fragment within a very complex genome, a bacterial cell, a human cell, or a fruit-fly cell.

The length of that oligonucleotide is determined by the number of genes that cell has. A small virus, such as the phage lamda that infects bacterial cells, has about fifty genes and about 50,000 base pairs of DNA. In contrast, the haploid human genome, that one metre of DNA I mentioned, contains about three billion base pairs and probably encodes about 100,000 genes. What we see when we look at one another is not the DNA that we inherited from our parents, but the products of those genes, most of the product being protein. It's skin, muscle, cartilage, hair, and hormones, such as growth hormone that determines size or hormones such as insulin that determine metabolism. It's enzymes that digest food and enzymes that build up muscle and other organs and tissues. That is what you're producing, and the more complex you are, the more of those proteins you need. But even with human DNA the average length of an oligonucleotide needed to recognize a specific gene is approximately seventeen bases long. For the yeast Saccharomyces Cerevisiae, the length is about thirteen bases.

We wanted to investigate this possibility of using oligonucleotides to isolate sequence, so we had to do a series of model studies. No one really knew in 1968 how specific a duplex (a pair of DNA strands) could be between an oligonucleotide and a DNA complementary to it. We made these simple chemical entities by the Khorana method, doing a form of affinity chromatography — by measuring the ability of a duplex to form, and measuring its stability by the temperature at which we could dissociate a duplex that had been formed at low temperature. We were able to show that a duplex that was nine base pairs long had a different stability from one that was eight base pairs long, or one that was ten base pairs long. Furthermore, a perfectly matched duplex was more stable than one with a mismatch. (Although, even if we have a mismatch in a short duplex at low temperature, we could form a Watson-Crick structure with a little loop in the middle.)

This kind of experimentation, which took four or five years, encouraged us to believe that we could use a synthetic oligonucleotide to recognize a naturally occurring piece of nucleic acid in a completely specific way. But we needed to know the sequence of the target DNA before we could synthesize a fragment to recognize it; it's the chicken-and-egg situation. We had an entry, however: the amino acid sequence of a protein and a particular class of mutation called double-frame shift mutants, where a nucleotide is deleted from a DNA in one place and, later on down the DNA coding sequence, another one is inserted. The amino acid sequence of the normal gene would read a particular amino acid sequence. The amino acid sequence of the mutant protein would start off the same as the wild type, but when it comes to the point where the nucleotide is deleted, it starts encoding different amino acids because we've frameshifted the codons (a group of three nucleotides that encode an amino acid) by one nucleotide. When we come to the place where another nucleotide has been inserted, we get back in the reading frame, and the next amino acid is the same as the wild type. So, by looking at the amino acid sequence, we can resolve a problem that is intrinsic to DNA encoding of proteins where the code is degenerate. Since there is more than one triplet codon for each amino acid, amino acid sequence alone doesn't unambiguously tell us a DNA sequence. But if we compare the two amino acid sequences and the partial predictions of code from the two of them, we can unambiguously predict a particular sequence between the deletion and the insertion.

When we started this work in the early 1960s it was difficult to make an oligonucleotide. The task of making one thirteen bases long would take us eight or nine months, given the technologies available. Today, scientists can buy a machine, press a button, and sixty minutes later have their oligonucleotide. We used that oligonucleotide and we were able to get the gene we wanted, that of cytochrome c from yeast. Again, it gets back to this issue of the library where you've got, in the case of yeast, several thousand different colonies of bacteria, each with a different piece of yeast DNA and, if you can pull the two strands of the DNA apart, which you can do by heating them, you can add the oligonucleotides and isolate the piece of DNA that your probe recognizes. However, you still need to confirm that you have the gene you want. The only way you can find out is by determining the DNA sequence.

In 1975 I had the good fortune to go to Fred Sanger's lab in Cambridge. Sanger is one of four individuals who have won two Nobel Prizes, the others being Marie Curie, who won a physics and a chemistry prize; Linus Pauling, who won a chemistry and a peace prize; and John Bardeen, who won two physics prizes. Sanger won two chemistry prizes. He was working on the nucleotide sequence of the DNA of a small virus. It was unusual in that it replicated its DNA in an infected bacterial cell as the circular double-stranded molecule, but when the mature phage, a virus which infects a bacterium, was made, it packaged only one of those strands as a single-stranded circle in the particle. Since it was single-stranded DNA, Sanger could take a short DNA fragment, anneal it to that single-stranded DNA, and use that short fragment as a primer to make a copy of the template enzymatically, the long strand of the virus. The basic principle is fairly simple. A long, naturally occurring piece of DNA strand is a template for DNA polymerase, and a short fragment annealed to it is a primer for the enzyme.

A normal synthesis would end by making a double-stranded molecule. What Sanger did was develop a method where in one particular experiment, say wherever it said A, the new strand in the template stopped growing. If you did four experiments, wherever there was an A, some of the chains stopped growing; where there was a T, some of the chains stopped growing; and in a third with Cs and a fourth with Gs, you would have four different set mixtures of compounds. Those could be put in an apparatus that separates the negatively charged molecules, or DNA, according to size by passing them through a gel, the smaller fragments moving faster and the larger ones moving more slowly. You then get what is called an interrupted ladder pattern. By just looking at the lengths — the shortest first and gradually going to the longest — we can figure out the sequence of the DNA.

There were two strokes of genius in Sanger's work. First, he contravened the basic tenets of organic chemists, who were always trying to get reactions to go with a 100 percent yield. If he had done that, he would have stopped at the first A or the first G or the first C. His experiment was designed so that 99 percent of the time it did not stop, and so he got many fragments. Many chemists would not have thought of doing that because their culture said you go for high yields, and Sanger's method required low yields. The other thing he recognized was that in gel electrophoresis you could actually separate molecules that might differ by masses of just 300, which is roughly the mass of a nucleotide, in a basic background mass of about 30,000 or 50,000. In other words, the resolving power of the gel electrophoresis was phenomenal. No one knew that. It was an accidental discovery, and it led to this truly revolutionary method.

To give an example of what a revolution it was, Erwin Chargaff, the man who did the work on DNA analysis that led to the idea of base pairing, wrote an article in 1968 on the current state of DNA sequence determination. In that article, he said current technology means that the first genome we can totally sequence, which contains about 5,000 base pairs out of a small virus, will take until the middle of the next century, by which time we will have other problems. He was wrong in his prediction because the total sequence of ØX 174, which is just over 5,000 nucleotides, was done within nine years because of the amazing effect of this nonlinear change in technology that Sanger's methodology provided. I learned to DNA sequence in Sanger's laboratory by being one of the team working on the sequence of this virus.

Another surprising and unpredictable outcome was that the same piece of DNA had overlapping genes within it. It could encode two different proteins. That was possible because the code was a triplet and we could read the amino acid protein sequence by starting at nucleotide 1, and then going 1, 4, 7, 10, and 13. Or we could read a different protein from the same DNA by starting at 2, and going 2, 5, 8, 11, 14, and so forth. No one had any idea that would happen. Theoretically it was possible, but no one thought it would actually occur because of the constraints that the three-dimensional structure of a protein would put on what could be coded, making it impossible for two functional proteins to be encoded by the same piece of DNA.

This is one of the reasons I've always been a strong advocate of a genomic program; you find information about the organism you want to study from its DNA's sequence, which is not accessible, either from genetics or from biochemistry. It also made me realize that if we were going to resolve the genetics of an organism such as this, we needed a precise genetic tool that would go to a particular nucleotide and make a particular genetic change. We'd observed that you could form a duplex with a short oligonucleotide, even if there was a non-Watson-Crick match there. It brings us to the point that other people had thought it was important to have a good genetic methodology. Joshua Lederberg in his Nobel Prize acceptance speech pointed out that there was a need for a specific tool that would make a specific change in a specific gene. He had to speculate, against the background of known biology in 1958, when genetics was done on the intact genomes of living organisms. After that time, the whole set of tools I've talked about was developed, leading to genetic engineering where we could take a gene, put it in a test tube, do something to it, and put it back in the living cell. That changed the ball game.

Using the synthetic oligonucleotide, we can form a structure, a Watson-Crick structure, with a mismatch and yield to a naturally occurring circular nucleic acid. Thereafter, it's fairly routine, using DNA polymerase and the joining enzyme, DNA ligase, to make a double-stranded molecule that is totally normal except at one place in one strand. If we put that molecule in a living cell, we can get it to replicate, and the template strand gives more normal progeny, while the strand with the oligonucleotide gives the specific mutant we hoped for. We tried this out in a very simple experiment using the ØX 174 DNA sequence, which had been determined in Sanger's laboratory, and we were able to show it would work. It was a wonderful and exciting experience to have that idea, which we discussed over cups of tea in the canteen that Dr. Perutz's wife used to manage in the MRC laboratory in Cambridge. The problem with ØX 174 was that it was a rather offbeat organism. It was interesting in its own right, but it wasn't a useful vector for other things. But biology is amazingly diverse, and E. coli, the bacteria that was a target of ØX 174, is also infected by other bacterial phages, including a category called filamentous phage.

We could also replicate circular double-stranded DNAs and packaged circular single strands. However, the filamentous phage is more adaptable than the ØX phage, so we could insert a piece of DNA into the circular double-stranded molecule and get it to package recombinant single-stranded DNA that makes a target for the same sort of experiment where you have a recombinant fragment in this viral vector. Again you make the molecule, which is circular, and you get progeny at the end, some of which are mutants, some of which are wild types. The problem here is, whereas in ØX 174 we were able to take advantage of the biology of the virus to recognize the mutant because it had a phenotype, or something you could see in the cell, if you put a foreign gene in an E. coli cell, there is no phenotype, nothing you can see, so you have to go and look for the mutant DNA. This is where the oligonucleotides again proved useful.

If we have a perfectly matched oligonucleotide, it will form a stable structure. If there's a mismatch, it is less stable. The oligonucleotide that was used to make the mutation should therefore perfectly recognize mutant DNA, whereas it will form a less than perfect structure with wild type DNA. The mutagenic oligonucleotide, labelled with radioactivity, annealed at a low temperature to the different colonies, or plaques in this case, of phage on E. coli will detect all the DNA. Warmed up to a higher temperature, it gets washed off the wild type DNA but stays stuck to the mutant. That is the ultimate development of the methodology. It was completed in about 1982. Since that time, it has been improved in efficiency by a number of other groups.

Most people are using oligonucleotide-based site-directed mutagenesis for studying how proteins work. Other researchers are using it to modify proteins, and still others use it to produce recombinately produced proteins. Insulin, which was discovered by Frederick Banting, J. J. R. MacLeod, Charles Best, and J. B. Collip in Toronto in the early 1920s, is produced in the human pancreas. What was used to treat people for many years was insulin isolated either from beef pancreas or pig pancreas, and that worked, but there were problems. It's an unreliable source of raw material, the purification is difficult, and you can have immune reactions because the protein from these animals is not exactly the same as the human one. Recombinant DNA technology made it possible to take the human gene and put it into a microorganism.

The gene is fairly complex. It has a signal to start making messenger RNA and to stop making messenger RNA, a signal to say secrete, a peptide that helps the two chains of the protein — the A chains and the B chains — to form up correctly and later be removed. You can't just move that from humans to yeast, for instance. You have to put a yeast signal to start making messenger RNA, a yeast signal to stop making it. You have to put a yeast signal to say secrete it, and you have to put a modified peptide in to bring the two chains together. But this can be done, and this oligonucleotide technology I mention can be used not only to make specific changes in DNA, but to join bits together precisely, to insert bits, and to eliminate bits. And now the sources of human insulin are E. coli or yeast, and there are many other examples.

Now, if I wasn't here telling you about this development, it would be someone else who had done the same thing. But there were two crucial factors that led to my doing it. One was having a man like Ned Steacie at an influential level in government, who made a decision that it was important for this country to fund basic research. Second, was having a man like Gordon Shrum, who knew that it was essential to recruit the very best people, and to let them do what they thought was best.

CHRISTIAN RENÉ DE DUVE

Nobel Prize in Medicine or Physiology, 1974

$\mathcal{T}$*he survival of an organism depends on the relationship between a cell and its subcellular structure. Christian de Duve's research has focused on the separation and characterization of the different parts, called organelles, of living cells. For "discoveries concerning the structural and functional organization of the cell," he, with Albert Claude and George E. Palade, was awarded the Nobel Prize for medicine or physiology in 1974. De Duve is best known for his 1955 discovery of a new cell part, the lysosome, which functions as the cell's digestive system. He made the discovery using centrifugation for separating cell parts.*

Trained as an M.D. and later as a chemist, de Duve became involved in research because of an interest in the action mechanism of insulin, the hormone that regulates the body's use of sugar. With this goal in mind, he focused on certain enzymatic aspects of metabolism in the liver. "But fate had a surprise in store for me, in the form of a chance observation, the so-called latency of acid phosphatase. It was essentially irrelevant to the object of our research but it was most intriguing. My curiosity got the better of me, and as a result I never elucidated the mechanism of action of insulin. I pursued my accidental finding."

Since the discovery of lysosomes, de Duve and his group have made numerous contributions to the development of techniques and instrumentation for cell biology. They are also responsible for the discovery of peroxisomes, organelles involved in the metabolism of fat.

Born in England in 1917, where his Belgian parents were taking refuge during the First World War, de Duve received his education at the University of Louvain, Belgium. He shares his time between the Rockefeller University in New York and the University of Louvain. He is founder of the International Institute of Cellular and Molecular Pathology in Brussels. His recent interests are in the origin and evolution of life.

Christian René de Duve with his wife, Janine

LIFE AS A
COSMIC IMPERATIVE

*W*hat is life? How did it come about? Does it have any meaning? How do we fit within its general scheme? These are questions that have traditionally been addressed by philosophers and theologians, but in recent years they have become concerns for scientists as well. The knowledge we have acquired — and continue to acquire — concerning the nature of life and its evolution has provided us with more information than philosophers have on which to base rational and meaningful answers to these questions.

Many advances have been made in our understanding of life's most intimate processes. The history of life is written in the molecules and cells of living beings, and we are becoming increasingly proficient at reading the text. Much of it is still blurred, however, and scientists still quarrel about interpretations, influenced in part by their areas of expertise and sometimes by their ideological biases. I wish to tell you how I, as a biochemist and cell biologist, read and interpret the text. A detailed view is offered in my recent book, *Vital Dust: Life as a Cosmic Imperative*.[1]

First, what is life? Much has been written on this question, including the influential book of the same title published fifty years ago by the celebrated physicist Erwin Schrödinger. My own answer to this question is that life is what is common to all living beings. My definition is not a tautology, because it allows us to exclude a large number of properties from the definition. To be alive, a being need not have green leaves, or wings, or a shell, or hands. It need not even have many cells. Many living beings consist of single cells, some of which, like the bacteria, or prokaryotes (primitive single cells), are 10,000 times smaller in volume than our own cells and are endowed with a much more rudimentary organization. Life is what remains after all differences are disregarded. It is what is common among a plague bacillus, a yeast cell, an amoeba, a toadstool, a fern, a fox, and a human being.

All living beings are made of the same basic constituents: proteins, nucleic acids, carbohydrates, fats, and so on. All living beings use the same, or similar, chemical pathways to build their constituents, metabolize foodstuffs, and produce energy. All living beings use the same basic mechanisms to retrieve energy and convert it into work. All living beings use the same language, the same genetic code. In fact, these similarities are so strong that we can now state with assurance that all living organisms are descendants from a single ancestral form of life.

Particularly convincing proof of this assertion comes from the sequence similarities among proteins that perform the same function in different organisms, and among the genes that code for these proteins. These similarities provide unmistakable evidence that the molecules are descendants from a single ancestral form that evolved in slightly different ways, because some mutations changed the sequence without destroying the biological activity of the molecule. This technique of comparative sequencing has become a major tool for reconstructing the pathways of evolution.

Imagine yourself in a world where words change by copying

mistakes. Suppose you are comparing languages and you find a word in one area spelled *professor*, but in another it is spelled *processor*. You know that words evolve and change by means of copying mistakes, so you can assume that these two words originate from a common ancestral word. The letter *f* may have been changed to *c*, or vice versa. Then you find another two words, such as *protector* and *projector*. Again, you can assume that these are descendants from a single ancestral form. Comparing the four words, you can go back a little further in time and say that all four are descendants from a common ancestor that has the letters *p*, *r*, *o*, *e*, and *o*, *r* in common.

This, in a very simplistic way, illustrates the strength of this molecular sequencing technique for reconstructing evolution. The whole history of life is written into the sequences of our proteins and nucleic acids, and by analysing living organisms it is possible to go back to the common ancestor of all life on Earth.

Now to my second question: How did life come about? From what we have just seen, this question may be reworded: How did the common ancestor of all life come about? Even thus simplified, the problem remains a daunting one, far from being solved. But there are clues. They come from outer space, from the Earth's crust, from laboratory experiments, and especially from extant organisms. Time does not allow me to give even an elementary survey of the many facts and ideas that have been collected on the subject of the origin of life. Let me simply make a few points of a very general nature.

First, life arose naturally. This is a postulate. Life arose spontaneously by processes entirely explainable in terms of physics and chemistry. If I do not accept this postulate, the origin of life ceases to be a scientific problem and my presentation has no sense. This statement excludes creationism, the name given to literal interpretation of the biblical account for the beginning of life. It also excludes vitalism, a doctrine that was popular a century ago. Vitalism is the belief that living organisms are made of matter animated by some kind of vital spirit or force. This definition also excludes finalism, a doctrine that assumes that living organisms not only are driven by antecedent causes — phenomena that have occurred before and that push them — but are pulled by some kind of purpose. For instance, a finalistic view of the stomach is to say that the stomach evolved for digesting food. The scientific way is to say that the stomach is an organ capable of digesting food. There's a difference. We remove the purpose, even though we know that living organisms behave as though they were accomplishing a purpose.

Life arose naturally, and it did so by way of chemical processes. The processes underlying life are all essentially chemical, and virtually everything that happens in living organisms is based on chemical interaction and reaction. The great conquests of modern biology are essentially a growing ability to explain life's fundamental properties in molecular terms. If life arose naturally, it must have done so by a succession of chemical processes leading from simple molecular building blocks to macromolecular and polymolecular assemblages of increasing complexity.

This leads to the third statement; life arose through a very large number of successive steps. One can't assume that a living cell or even a molecule of DNA would emerge at one time. The British astronomer Sir Fred Hoyle made the point well. He said a Boeing 747 cannot arise spontaneously, ready to fly, from a junkyard swept by a hurricane. A living cell is much more complicated than a Boeing 747.

The nature of the steps involved is the object of much work and of even more speculation and controversy. I shall not bother with details but would like simply to state a personal view, not widely shared by experts in the field but resting on what I believe to be a solid argument. According to this view, the early steps that led to the first nucleic acids, proteins, and other major biological constituents were not very different from the steps that make those same molecules in extant organisms. To clarify the issue, let me call protometabolism the set of early chemical reactions whereby life arose and was sustained until the present machinery of genes and enzymes became operative. I'll call the set of enzyme-catalyzed reactions that were developed later, and still support living organisms today, metabolism. For obvious reasons, the transition from protometabolism to metabolism cannot have been abrupt. Most likely, it took place by the stepwise appearance — as a result of some mutational event — of single new enzymes, each of which catalyzed a reaction that turned out to be useful and was therefore retained by natural selection. This explanation implies that the new enzyme fitted within the protometabolic network: that it found in the network one or more substances on which to act and an outlet for its products. Let this reasoning be extended to the hundreds of distinct enzymes that were progressively acquired in the course of the transition, and the inference follows that protometabolism and metabolism were congruent — that they followed similar pathways.

Irrespective of the nature of the steps involved, one last statement may safely be made: with rare possible exceptions, all the innumerable steps in the long pathway from simple chemical building blocks to the first cells had a very high probability of taking place under the prevailing conditions. They were virtually bound to occur under those conditions, and they should similarly occur anywhere and any time the same conditions obtain. This strongly deterministic view of the origin of life contrasts with that defended by a number of scientists who have claimed that life is the product of a highly improbable combination of circumstances, so improbable, in fact, that it may be unique in the history of the universe and could very well never have happened at all. As the late Jacques Monod stated in his 1970 bestseller *Chance and Necessity*, "The universe was not pregnant with life."[2]

To support their view of life as a highly improbable event, Monod and others point out that highly improbable events occur all the time without our being aware. When four players gather around a bridge table and take up their cards, they witness a distribution that has one chance in 50 billion billion billion of being dealt. Nevertheless, bridge players hardly ever exclaim at being witness to an extraordinary event when they take up their cards. They do so only when there is something special about the distribution. They would certainly rave if, say, each player should pick up all thirteen cards of a given suit: one player all thirteen spades, another all thirteen diamonds, another all thirteen hearts, and the last all thirteen clubs. But such a distribution is no more improbable than any other. Every time a hand is dealt, it has probably never been dealt before, and may never be dealt in the foreseeable future. Such, it is said, could have been the case also of the emergence of life, a single event of infinitesimally small probability that happened to take place by an extraordinary combination of circumstances, a cosmic fluke, not likely to be repeated anywhere or any time in the universe.

This argument is impeccable as long as it applies to a single event. But life arose by a succession of a very large number of steps. We're not dealing with thirteen spades, hearts, diamonds, and clubs once, but twice, ten times, a hundred times, a million times in succession. This is strictly impossible unless the deck is doctored. In the case of life, a doctored deck means a universe pregnant with life. Life must obligatorily arise wherever conditions are suitable. Life is a cosmic imperative.

The possibility remains, however, that the required set of conditions has an extremely low probability of ever being realized. If this were so, life, even though the product of a highly deterministic sequence of events, would still have an extremely low probability of arising. Although pregnant with life, the universe would have almost no chance of ever delivering, because of the extremely low probability of the conditions needed for bringing the pregnancy to a successful conclusion. The appearance of life would still be a cosmic fluke.

This objection won't be answered until there exists proof of life having arisen independently elsewhere in the universe, or evidence that the conditions elsewhere are suitable for life. Or it may never be answered. The consensus of the experts is that our planet is not so extraordinary, and that the physical and chemical history of Earth is being or has been or will be repeated in many other places in the universe. An estimate of one million planets capable of bearing life per galaxy has been suggested as reasonable. Even if this estimate is off by several orders of magnitude, that still implies billions of living planets.

Is it thinking, conscious life? There is more than one way of looking at the tree of life. One can see a wonderful canopy with millions of twigs and leaves, representing the extraordinary diversity of life on Earth. What strikes many evolutionary biologists in this spectacle is its contingency. If it were to start all over again, the result would not be the same canopy, because so many factors are involved in the bifurcations, the branchings, that give more and more different twigs. In this view, the human species is just one among a million twigs, "only an afterthought," as Stephen Jay Gould puts it in *Wonderful Life*, "a kind of cosmic accident, just one bauble on the Christmas tree of evolution."[3]

Trim the tree of its canopy, however, and what you see is the trunk. As life progresses, there is a rise towards increasing complexity — from bacteria to the higher plants in one line, to the higher animals in the other. Here, the human twig occupies the top of the trunk — at least provisionally. Ten million years from now, another species more advanced than we are could be at the top. There are reasons for believing that there are constraints that force life towards greater complexity. The trunk of the tree of life could owe much less to contingency that its canopy.

Jacques Monod derived a despairing philosophy of life. In the last sentence of his book he writes: "Man knows at last that he is alone in the universe's unfeeling immensity, out of which he emerged only by chance. His destiny is nowhere spelled out; nor is his duty." My interpretation of the data leads to a more hopeful philosophy, a more meaningful universe.

NOTES
1 C. de Duve, *Vital Dust: Life as a Cosmic Imperative* (New York: Basic Books, 1995).

2 J. Monod, *Le hasard et la nécessité* (Paris: Éditions du Seuil, 1970); *Chance and Necessity*, English translation by A. Wainhouse (New York: Knopf, 1971).

3 S. J. Gould, *Wonderful Life* (New York: Norton, 1989).

PART III

THE NEXT HALF-CENTURY

HENRY WAY KENDALL

Nobel Prize in Physics, 1990

*E*lementary particles, basic building blocks of atoms, hold our universe together. Henry Kendall, with Jerome Friedman and Richard Taylor, examined subatomic-level interactions at the Stanford Linear Accelerator Center (SLAC) in the 1960s through electron-scattering experiments. Electron scattering involves bombarding atoms with high-speed electrons and observing them after the collision. The faster the incoming electrons, the farther they can penetrate into the atoms and the more information scientists can glean. This research led to a better understanding of elementary particles' internal structures and to the 1990 Nobel Prize in physics for providing evidence of these very small particles.

It was during his time at Stanford that Kendall became concerned about the effects of science on society, earning him the nickname "the conscience of science." He became involved in science policy in the early 1960s when, troubled by the buildup of nuclear arsenals, he joined a group of scientists advising the U.S. Defense Department. He was also *a founding member of the Union of Concerned Scientists in 1969, a powerful public interest group that lobbies for control of potentially harmful technologies. It is also an avenue through which scientists take responsibility for research-spawned technology. The group has played an important role in several controversial issues such as nuclear reactor safety, the strategic defence initiative, and the greenhouse effect. He became director of the organization in 1974.*

Kendall was born in Boston in 1926, and has been a faculty member at the Massachusetts Institute of Technology since 1961. A man of eclectic interests, his first books on shallow-water diving and underwater photography were written from his experience in managing a diving and salvage operation during his college years. He also enjoys rock climbing and mountaineering, and has joined expeditions to the Himalayas, the Andes, and the Arctic.

Henry Way Kendall

GLOBAL
PROSPECTS

*T*wo colleagues and I shared the
Nobel Prize a few years back for the experimental discovery of
quarks, the basic building blocks of matter. That was, and
remains, the purest kind of basic research. Basic research was
defined for us some years ago by a former U.S. secretary of
defense who said that even if basic research is successful, nobody
gets anything from it — humorous, but far from correct.

I've also had a great interest in research that is not basic, on
problems of great relevance to those of us now living and to
future generations. These problems relate to environmental damage, resource management and mismanagement, and population
growth. It's a cluster of problems growing in importance which
will be with us for a long time. My interest in these areas does
not involve academic research, but lies in participating in the
political process to see remediation move forward to solve, or at
least ameliorate, these problems.

In recent years, colleagues in the scientific community and I have been trying to get a synoptic view, a general idea, of where human activities in these areas are taking us. We have been attempting to take action, because humanity's current course is disastrous. Our goals are expansive and, since they take in many human activities, there's always the risk that we are overreaching and that the goal is too big to be accomplished.

In 1991, the year after my colleagues and I had won the prize, the Nobel Foundation organized a jubilee at the time of the awards to celebrate their ninetieth anniversary. They invited all the living winners of the prize to Stockholm and put on a number of interesting extra activities, one of which was the Great Nobel Debate between two teams of laureates. Archbishop Desmond Tutu and I were the two spokespersons for the groups, the proposition being, "Is the human race using its collective intelligence to build a better world?" Being a somewhat garrulous professor and having a well-known position on this topic, I ended up speaking for the No team, and Archbishop Tutu spoke for the Yes team. When we compared notes, we each agreed with the other's position. I was talking about resource management and environmental injury, while his position was based on the great improvements that followed from the demise of apartheid and the fragmentation of the Soviet Union.

Preparing for that debate was, for me, a daunting experience. The subject was not, and is not, my professional field, so I launched into it some months early by talking to a number of senior scientists in the world community, principally biologists but also climatologists and atmospheric chemists, to try to consolidate my understanding of this nest of problems and the impact human activities had on them. I forged ahead in a way that reminded me of a newspaper masthead published in Boston during the revolutionary war. It said, "Often in error, never in doubt." Two things emerged from my study that surprised and unsettled me: the first was that the community of biologists, not so much microbiologists but population experts, ecologists, population dynamics people, demographers, and those who deal with the larger aspects of biology and the natural world, were enormously upset — distraught — by the massive loss of species and by what is happening to the natural world and the biosphere. They regarded it as tampering with the complex web of life on an enormous scale and leaving unintentional damage as the by-product of other activities. This anxiety communicated itself to me.

After the Nobel debate wound down, my colleagues and I in the Union of Concerned Scientists came to believe that the senior scientific community was probably ready to speak out on these issues because so many of us were upset at what was happening. We organized a declaration that we sent to senior members of the global scientific community, National Academy of Science-level people throughout the world. It was modestly entitled "World Scientists' Warning to Humanity." It's a long document, but I would like to quote the first few lines. "Human beings and the natural world are on a collision course. Human activities inflict harsh and often irreversible damage on the environment and on critical resources. If not checked, many of our current practices put at serious risk the future that we wish for human society, the plant and animal kingdoms, and may so alter the living world that it will be unable to sustain life in the manner that we know."

The document was signed by the largest group of senior scientists in the world ever to speak out on this issue, including a majority of both the Nobel Prize winners in the sciences and the Pontifical Academy of Sciences, even though it directly addresses the population issue and the necessity for stabilizing population growth. It also garnered signatures from across the industrial world and the Third World, bridging the often acrimonious gap as to the source of our troubles. The signers included many people who ordinarily do not sign things, such as the head officers of senior professional and honorary societies, the president and the secretary general of the Royal Swedish Academy of Sciences, the head of the Chinese Academy, the head of the Royal Society of London, and a number of senior officers of Canada's societies. It's a warning that comes from the community which is best able, through skill, experience, and knowledge, to address the structural problems and the environmental problems we face.

The title of my article, "Global Prospects," is somewhat diffuse, and I'm going to restrict it to a few narrow issues. Many human activities carried out on an enormous scale are putting huge pressure on the global systems that are crucial to us. We have already injured the world's atmosphere. We've altered it, changed it, with respect to CO_2, and to ultraviolet radiation balance, which is related to the ozone layer, resulting in the transmission of biologically damaging ultraviolet radiation to ground level. There is much ground-level pollution, particularly from urban areas. It stems mainly from energy-related activities and from burning fossil fuels, whose effluent spreads out and has the capacity to injure many things, among them agricultural productivity. We are cutting down the world's forests, particularly the tropical rain and dry forest, but the temperate forest as well. Land, especially arable land and food growing resources, is under terrible destructive pressure. Problems in the marine environment are well known to Canadians: overfishing, and coastal pollution from municipal and agricultural operations and industrial releases. These pollutants enter the coastal zone, where most of the food fish and most species spend part of their lives, particularly in spawning. The pressures on the world's fisheries are enormous. The United Nations has noted that for the seventeen major world fisheries, every one is either fully exploited, in decline, or approaching collapse. Canada, and now the United States, are witnessing the collapse of the eastern fisheries. The western salmon fisheries are going the same route. There is great pressure on fresh water supplies globally. In some eighty countries, 40 percent of the world's population lives in areas that are already chronically short of water. Lastly, and in a sense most important, food supplies are under great pressure because of widespread harsh agricultural practices, both in the Third World and in the industrial nations. The population of the world has expanded to the point where there is not much potentially arable land left to expand into, and what is available is of much lower quality than what is already cultivated. In Asia, for example, 80 percent of the potentially arable land is already under cultivation. Water supplies, which are vital for irrigation, are short and per capita food production in the world, rising for many years as a result of the green revolution, now appears to have climaxed and has started a decline. The per capita arable land in the world is currently decreasing at about the same rate that the population is increasing. And finally, population. We stand today at roughly 5.7 billion people. Fertility has declined somewhat in recent years, yet not enough. The momentum inherent in the population growth means a record ninety-odd million people are added every year, equivalent to the full population of Mexico.

Let me talk about the near future. Mark Twain remarked that it was difficult to make predictions, particularly about the future. I won't risk that, but I will consider where current trends will take us if they continue. In other words, what does "business as usual" for a few decades mean? It means great trouble. Today, according to the United Nations and the World Bank, one person in five does not get enough to eat and lives in what they call absolute poverty. One person in ten suffers from serious malnutrition, a disease from which you do not recover if it starts early in life. Food shortages loom if troubles arising from a long list of bad agricultural practices, in particular erosion and other environmental matters, are not corrected. Distribution problems account for some of the malnutrition; food shortages are not entirely to blame. If corrective measures are not taken, these matters are slated to get worse, and will unhinge countries where they are an underlying problem: Rwanda, Somalia, nearly two dozen other nations in Africa, some countries in the Middle East, Latin America, south Asia, and in Haiti, where erosion has swept large areas of that unhappy land free of soil, leaving sterile boulder fields.

If things continue as they are, the fish are going to disappear. It's not widely understood that fish are not an important source of food, providing between only 1 and 2 percent of human food. If they disappear, some coastal nations will suffer serious consequences, but the global food supplies would not be affected in a significant way. The industry based on natural fish does not have the potential to be much bigger than it is now. But the loss will be a loss for other reasons, reasons that relate to the disruption of delicate environmental chains.

The loss of rainforests brings with it the principal, but by no means the only, destruction of species. It is also not widely known that between two-thirds and maybe as much as 80 percent of the deforestation in the tropics, dry and wet, is for the purpose of producing arable land for hungry people who need to grow food. Unless the food problem can be solved, the rainforests are doomed, and with them numerous species. The loss of species is proceeding at a rate that has not been known for millions of years. Species diversity is now as low as it has been in sixty million years, and we are slated to lose an estimated 30 percent of living species by the end of the next century unless something is done. That, in round numbers, is the future, under business as usual. The unhinging and unsettling of countries that run short of food and whose environmental destruction will increasingly spawn refugees — a flow that is already in the tens of millions — is a problem of untold magnitude for both the industrial and the developing world.

Let me talk about an alternative future where the human race does not go this route. If we move to control environmental damage in a much broader and more powerful way, and go back to repair as much of the previous damage as we can, manage our resources more frugally and carefully, and treat waste more thoughtfully, we will have started to control the troubling activities. However, the world's population growth, according to demographers, is such that we will see our numbers doubled by the middle of the next century, in about fifty-five years. Barring some unforeseen catastrophe, we will likely reach a population in the vicinity of 10 billion people, with almost all of that growth occurring in the developing world. The industrial nations are at present at 1 billion people out of 5.7 billion, and the projections suggest that this number will grow to 1.2 billion in approximately sixty years. In the same period, the developing world will grow to 9 billion. If that growth is not stabilized, it will be an absolute obstacle to controlling the damage to the world's systems from environmentally injurious activities, much of which is irreversible. This is the link between environmental injury and population.

We cannot control damage to the world if we do not stabilize population. This message is brought to you by the scientific community. In the United States, and I suspect in Canada and in Europe as well, many people think of the population problem as being a distant one in some Third World nation, unconnected with environmental concerns: "It's probably their own fault, too, but it's not our problem." I can make a good case that in North America we have a population problem of our own, and that this one is, to some extent, our fault, and, to a very considerable extent, our responsibility. The developing nations must realize that the most serious threat they face is environmental damage that cannot be controlled if their populations continue growing at the rate they are. The industrial world — North America, Europe, Japan, a few of the Asian tigers — must control its overconsumption. The United States is the world's largest polluter, and has made reckless use of its resources and been highly irresponsible with waste disposal. We in the industrial world must realize that we have a responsibility to the Third World. First of all, we are all in one lifeboat, and it is not true that only one end of the boat can sink. We are the nations that have the intellectual resources, the scientific and engineering skills, the financial resources, to provide what is needed in the food sector, the energy sector, and elsewhere. We must help the Third World nations reduce their pervasive poverty, which is such an enormous problem, and to provide family planning services, contraceptive devices, education, and empowerment of women. Women in the Third World not only raise the families, but have, in many countries, major agricultural responsibility as well. Education of women is vital. With knowledge and equipment, they can help take better care of the land, and that is an enormously urgent goal to achieve.

Two elements might play a role in accomplishing our goals. First, what about the environmental movement? Why isn't it enough to do the job? It is big and powerful, and it cannot be reversed: between 1960 and 1985 more than three dozen major pieces of environmental legislation in the United States changed the scene completely. Yet there is something interesting about the environmental movement, if you look at it in detail.

In order to change legislation, environmentalists had to change the government's views on things. Where did the political force behind the environmental movement and the activists come from? It came from felt injury; from sewage on the beaches, polluted water supplies, air you couldn't see through that brought on coughing spells. People were upset and angry, and the resulting political force was what the environmental movement helped organize and guide in bringing about constructive changes through corrective legislation. This process is not restricted to the environmental movement. It's the path the civil rights movement and the women's movement followed. It's how revolutions start. First the injury, then the response. But we have no experience in dealing with the kinds of problems I'm talking about, with long-range problems that are predictable for the long run but where the injury is not already felt. We don't know how to raise the political force. We have to appeal to reason and that, unfortunately, often doesn't do well in the public domain. So we have a new sort of challenge facing us: the environmental movement has areas where it has power and can change things, but there are important problems that escape the net. The fisheries is one. It was known for years that overfishing would injure the fish supply, but the environmental movement was unable to halt the damage, just as it is not able to deal effectively with the shortage and destruction of arable land and food. The community of environmentalists is an ally, but it hasn't the clout it needs.

Another consideration for meeting our goal is contributions from science and technology. It's what the Nobel laureates here deal with, what scientists and engineers deal with. There is a widely shared, interesting, and important misunderstanding, the belief that the underpinnings of our industrial society will somehow produce some magic bullets, some glittering achievements that will let us go on as we have been and will save us from the business-as-usual scenario I outlined. The scientific community does not believe that. It is implicit in the scientists' warning: there is no magic bullet that will let us continue the way we have. Do not misunderstand: science and technology are of enormous importance to present-day life. They are the life-support system for the technological society. Science and technology will play crucial roles in resolving our future problems in medicine, in changing the energy and other technologies we use across the board. But the problems we face are human problems, and they have to be dealt with differently. Science and technology did not save the fisheries. In fact, they enabled the fisheries to be destroyed, with searchlight sonar, with mile-long monofilament nets so effective at destruction they are known as curtains of death, with major offshore trawlers that vacuum the oceans. We need a new ethic, a new way of approaching the fragile world that is our home. Science can't rescue us without help.

We must initiate a much broader and more powerful environmental movement that can address those things untouched by the present movement and outside its grasp. We must control population and stabilize it. If we do not stabilize population in voluntary and humane ways, it will be done for us by nature, by natural processes, and it will be done brutally, as in Haiti, Somalia, and across Africa. If we do not control the environmental damage, much of which is irreversible or irreversible on a time scale of centuries, we will leave a ravaged and mutilated world to our children and our children's children. We do not have to go down this path. The future is, to a considerable extent, though not entirely, in our hands. The future is discretionary, and we can move towards a new ethic and convince political leaders, military leaders, and especially religious leaders of the seriousness of the problem. An important part of this problem is one of ethics, and not of gleaming devices and gadgets. Only then can we move into the future with the hope for the opportunities and advantages for succeeding generations that we now have for ourselves.

I remember an armed forces poster widely displayed during the First World War to recruit young Englishmen to engage in the slaughter that was then in progress. It was a striking poster with a picture of a stern-visaged Lord Kitchener, black mustache bristling and his finger pointed out with the caption, "I want you." My colleagues and I in the scientific community want you, as thoughtful, educated, intelligent people, to go out and help with this movement, to prevent the unfortunate future that otherwise lies ahead.

ILYA
PRIGOGINE

Nobel Prize in Chemistry, 1977

*I*lya Prigogine was going to be a criminal lawyer, but a book on the chemical composition of the brain altered his career plans. The text, which he came across while looking for books on criminal psychology, marked the start of a love affair with chemistry. Prigogine's research on the thermodynamics of solutions and other complex systems — thermodynamics being that branch of science dealing with the relationship between heat and other forms of energy — resulted in the Nobel Prize in chemistry in 1977. It was Prigogine's work on the formation of a non-equilibrium stationary state in solutions, particularly the theory of dissipative structures, that earned the Russian-born scientist the honour.

Fluid heated from below is less dense than the cooler liquid on top, and will therefore try to rise. The movement of the liquid is chaotic when the temperature differences between the top and the bottom liquid is small, but at a certain critical temperature difference the system spontaneously forms a regular hexagonal display of convection cells. In each cell, the liquid circulates from bottom to top and back. Prigogine named these states "dissipative structures" because, while they are the result of irreversible processes increasing entropy, they have a definite structure in space and time.

Born on January 25, 1917, just nine months before the Bolshevik Revolution, Prigogine's family left Moscow and spent some time in Lithuania and Berlin before settling in Brussels, Belgium. His academic career was spent primarily at the Université Libre de Bruxelles, where he received his undergraduate and graduate education, and in 1947 a professorship.

Prigogine founded the Ilya Prigogine Center for Studies in Statistical Mechanics at the University of Texas, Austin, and was appointed Regental Professor of Physics and Chemical Engineering at Texas. He divides his time between Belgium and the United States.

Ilya Prigogine

TIME, CHAOS, AND THE TWO CULTURES

The central parameter in non-equilibrium thermodynamics — time and some new perspectives about time — is not a new subject. Some 2,500 years ago, Heraclitus emphasized becoming and change, while Parmenides stressed being and considered reality to be static, claiming it is only on the surface that we see change.

This debate is still going on and has dominated Western thought. The problem of time forms the dividing line between what is now called "the two cultures." Karl Popper wrote a beautiful book called *The Open Universe: An Argument for Indeterminism,* in which he stated "the reality of time and change seems to me the crux of realism." Time is one of the recurrent themes of twentieth-century philosophy. You find it in Henri Bergson, Karl Popper, Alfred Whitehead, and Martin Heidegger. I find especially prophetic a short article by Bergson, "Le Possible et le Réel," in which he asks,

Why does reality flow? What is the use of time? Still, I say to myself "time is something"? It acts in a certain way. What can it do? The simple common-sense response is time is what prevents everything from happening in one stroke. It slows things down or rather, it is the essence of delay. Is it not the vehicle of creation and choice? Doesn't the existence of time prove that there is uncertainty in things? Isn't time itself synonymous with indeterminism?

According to Bergson, the existence of time implies that "things are not yet ready." But if things are not yet ready, then we are in some kind of state of preparation. The future is not given, which means that there is some kind of indeterminacy in nature.

This conclusion, as well as those of Heidegger and Whitehead, clashed with the view of the greatest physicist of the century, Albert Einstein, who repeatedly said that time as evolution is an illusion. And this conflict between the philosophical and the scientific view is one of the roots of the postmodernist criticism of science by Amélie Rorty and other philosophers who concluded that if science had so little to say about so fundamental a human dimension, then science could hold no great interest except for the scientist. It is interesting to analyse the origin of this controversy, for it lies in one of the basic characteristics of Western science: the formulation of laws of nature. Laws of nature — such as Newton's laws or Schrödinger's law or Einstein's laws — are deterministic and time reversible. In other words, if you change the direction of time, the equations still describe valid observations. They are deterministic because if you know the initial conditions, you can predict what will happen or what has happened in the past.

Let's compare this to our present view of the universe. In October 1994 *Scientific American* published a very interesting issue entitled "Life in the Universe." In it we find articles by Carl Sagan, Stephen Jay Gould, Martin Minsky, and others describing evolutionary patterns on all levels: in cosmology, in biology, in human societies, and so on. It is interesting to read what a great physicist like Steven Weinberg had to say on the subject:

"As much as we would like to take a unified view of nature, we keep encountering a stubborn duality in the role of intelligent life in the universe as both subject and student." He continues:

> On one hand, there is a Schrödinger equation which describes in a perfectly deterministic way how the wave function of any system changes with time. Then, quite separate, there is a set of principles that tells how to use the wave function to calculate the probabilities of various possible outcomes when someone makes the measurements.

I find this view difficult to accept. In it, the evolutionary patterns of the universe would be a result of our measurements. But we are children of time, and certainly not its father or mother. It is interesting to go a little further and to consider what the laws of physics might be in an evolutionary universe. Let me mention that we have inherited two conflicting views on the universe from the nineteenth century. One is the static view expressed by the laws of nature — Newton, Schrödinger, Einstein; the other is the second law of thermodynamics — the idea that entropy is an arrow of time — which describes an evolutionary universe. In other words, we have a contradiction. I have taught thermodynamics for many years and my best students are generally the students who come in to say, "What are you telling us? We have heard lectures about classical dynamics, quantum mechanics, and so on. We don't see anything like entropy present there. What is the meaning of entropy?" And that is a recurrent theme. If you look at recent books — for example, Stephen Hawking's *A Brief History of Time* or Murray Gell-Mann's *The Quark and the Jaguar*, you see that their way of trying to overcome this difficulty is to trivialize entropy. Gell-Mann goes so far as to say "entropy is ignorance." Likewise in the movie that was based on Hawking's book, somebody asks, "What is entropy?" Hawking's assistant takes a glass and throws it on the ground. The glass breaks and he says, "That is entropy. It is more probable that a glass is in many pieces than that it is in one piece." This is a very strange view of entropy. If this view of entropy were true, then only the breaking of glasses would be possible, and every time we produce a glass we would violate the second law. There would no longer be a second law.

I would like to discuss why this "entropy as ignorance" is no longer tenable. I will argue for the constructive role of time, and show that irreversibility is really an essential element in the formation of the complex structures in the world around us. Then I will consider the fundamental question, "What are the roots of time?" In conclusion, I will summarize some recent work that deals with instability, chaos, and a special form of chaos associated with what are called Poincaré resonances. These resonances are the basis of irreversibility; when they are included in classical or quantum mechanics, they result in a new formulation of the laws of classical and quantum mechanics, which includes probability and the arrow of time. In other words, in this form, the laws of nature no longer express certainty, but possibilities about things which may or may not happen. It is this form of physical laws that is appropriate to the evolving world in which we live.

First, a few words about thermodynamics. An important step along the path was the introduction of non-equilibrium thermodynamics some forty years ago. Through it, we understood that we had been too centred around equilibrium thermodynamics. In equilibrium thermodynamics, a system in equilibrium is stable. In other words, a system has attained maximum entropy or minimum free energy. If you perturb the system a little and the free energy goes up, it will go down again to the minimum. An equilibrium system is immune to its own fluctuations. When I first began to work in this field, I studied linear non-equilibrium situations, in which you are not far removed from equilibrium. Here again, a kind of stability reigns. If you perturb the system, it will come back to the initial state, which is characterized by minimum entropy production. But the surprise came later, when we tried to extend these results to systems far from equilibrium. Then something very unexpected happened. We found that there is no longer any potential which is minimum; that is, when we perturb the system, there is no longer any guarantee that the system will go back to its initial state. On the contrary, the system begins to explore new structures, new kinds of space-time organizations, which I called dissipative structures. It was clear that systems with conditions far from equilibrium are essential, because they lead to new structural aspects of matter. This outcome implies a new coherence, which leads, for example, to wave-like properties. Everybody has heard about oscillating chemical reactions in which all the molecules become blue together, then they all become red, and so on. This is amazing because to see this colour change, you need a coherent phenomenon involving billions of particles. Another example is the appearance of streams and vortexes, again far from equilibrium, where you see billions of particles working together, if I can be permitted to use this expression. This was really a big surprise. I described this behaviour by saying that near-equilibrium matter is blind; each molecule can see only its neighbours. Far from equilibrium, however, you have long-range correlations that are essential for building new structures. Work on dissipative structure is now very popular, and many laboratories all over the world are involved in it. New structures, spatial structures, self-reproducing structures, and the like are being discovered all the time. The idea of self-organization has also become very popular. Here, again, self-organization occurs because, when we are far from equilibrium, the system has many structural choices of which, in anthropomorphic language, it chooses one.

When I was young, my teachers were proud to show that a given problem had only one solution. But far from equilibrium, the equations representing a system have many equally good solutions and, in a sense, it is a fluctuation that decides which solution will prevail. Today we know under what conditions particular kinds of structures arise. We know that autocatalytic reactions — reactions that produce one of the reagents as a product so that the reagent concentration can actually increase (at least for a time) as the reaction proceeds — are involved. And we know that we must have non-linear chemical reactions. How, then, must thermodynamics be judged? What is the relation between thermodynamics and the basic laws of nature expressed by Newton? Let me quote a remark made by Henri Poincaré. In a short paper, Poincaré proved that classical dynamics and thermodynamics were incompatible. This led him to write:

> In conclusion, using ordinary language, the principle of Clausius, that is, the second law, can have only one meaning which is that it is a property common to all the possibilities; but according to the deterministic hypothesis there is only a single possibility and so the second law no longer has any meaning. According to the indeterministic hypothesis, on the other hand, it would be meaningful even if it were taken in an absolute sense; it would appear as a limitation imposed upon freedom. But these comments remind me that I am digressing, and I am on the point of leaving the domains of mathematics and physics.

I found this statement remarkable because Poincaré obviously understood that, in order to accommodate thermodynamics, we need some indeterminism, some statistical aspect in basic physics. But he found this idea so revolutionary that he recoiled in horror from it. Bergson arrived independently at this conclusion by philosophical considerations. I always wondered if Bergson had read Poincaré, and what Poincaré's opinion of Bergson was.

Today we can take Poincaré's suggestion seriously. We are able to show that instability can indeed lead to a modification of nature's basic laws. I will first explain this in terms of a very simple type of instability called deterministic chaos. In deterministic chaos, the basic laws are deterministic. Mathematicians have invented some simple systems, called maps, which illustrate the various forms of chaos. In a map, all numbers lie between 0 and 1. If you do something to a number which makes it greater than one, you can bring it back to the allowed interval by subtracting the integer portion. So multiplying 0.6 by 2 would give 1.2, which then becomes 0.2. This situation is reminiscent of the second hand of a clock, which always indicates a number between 0 and 60 however much time passes. There are two types of maps: stable periodic maps and unstable chaotic maps. You can get a stable periodic map by taking a number between zero and one, adding one-half every second. If you start with one-quarter, you get three-quarters, then five-quarters, but that is the same as one-quarter because you must go back to the interval between zero and one. The pattern then repeats itself and it is periodic. In contrast, you have chaotic maps, like the famous Bernoulli map, in which you multiply a number between zero and one by two and, if it exceeds one, you always bring it back to the interval between zero and one. You can show that if you take an arbitrary number, the arbitrary number is, generally speaking, an irrational number, and then in the series you get, the numbers fluctuate wildly between zero and one. This is a characteristic of chaos. In other words, in chaos the trajectories defined by two series of such numbers which began with two very close starting values can diverge. In fact, mathematicians have shown that they diverge exponentially. The distance between the trajectories increases proportional to the number of steps raised to an exponent, which is called the Lyapunov exponent.

Many computer scientists have noted that the situation changes when you start with a probability distribution of trajectories, rather than starting with a single trajectory. That is, you start with a continuous function that describes many trajectories. Then, contrary to the evolution of single trajectories, the evolution of the probability is very smooth and, for example, in the Bernoulli case, you rapidly attain a final limiting situation, which is a uniform distribution. This is a puzzle. When I look at the trajectories themselves, I cannot predict their future. However, if I look at probabilities, I can predict what the probability will do. That is really a very interesting situation, because, in a sense, I can learn more from the probabilities than from the individual data points. This has led to a mathematical theory that some of my young co-workers have been developing. With it, one no longer considers deterministic equations, but instead the effect of an operator, which is called the Perron-Frobenius operator, on the evolution of the probability with time. This problem is reminiscent of quantum mechanics, because as in quantum mechanics there are no trajectories but rather a wave function and operators acting on the wave function. However, there are fundamental mathematical differences between this theory and quantum mechanics. The latter is solved within what mathematicians call Hilbert space, but this solution is not applicable to probability distributions of chaotic trajectories because the functions involved are highly singular. They are not differentiable; they behave in a crazy way; they are fractals. As a result, one has to generalize functional analysis to encompass this type of situation, and only then can the problem be solved. But let me emphasize again, you solve the problem for probability distributions, but not for individual trajectories. Individual trajectories fluctuate wildly. You cannot see any order or pattern. Now this difference is very interesting, even from a philosophical point of view, because we see that we have to go beyond a description in terms of points. Classical physics or relativity is based on the idea that the fundamental object is a point. Here we have to take probability as the fundamental object. The classical idea was that probability is ignorance, that when we introduce probability we destroy all possibility of exact prediction. In a chaotic system, the situation is completely reversed. It is only by considering probability that you can predict what the temporal steps in the evolution of this function will be and how this function will reach a final asymptotic state.

This, I think, is the first example of an objective theory based on probability, not on probabilities as statements of ignorance but on probability because probability is the natural variable reflecting the complexity of the situation. Here, speaking of points is meaningless. Which point do you choose? One point goes left, a neighbouring point goes right. A point is not representative of the ensemble. By dealing with probability distributions directly, you obtain a theory that is probabilistic and time irreversible. It resembles the situation that prevails with the population of species, such as Darwin's theory of evolution, which operates on the level of the population but not on the level of individuals.

I would like to consider a second and much more important example that relates to real dynamical systems rather than to chaotic maps, which are, after all, simplified models of chaotic systems. Now I will deal with the real world. In the real world you also have two types of descriptions: one description is in terms of trajectories or wave functions — that is, an individual description; the second is a statistical description in which, again, probabilities are considered the basic elements. The question is, what is the relation between the two levels of description, the probabilistic description and the individual description? For simple systems, like harmonic oscillators, rotors, two-body problems, and so on, you can easily show that the two descriptions are equivalent. In other words, for all stable systems, if you start with a probabilistic description, you can go back to the individual level, and vice versa. If you solve the problem at the individual level, you can solve the probabilistic problem too. There is no difference. But there is a radical difference when you consider what Poincaré called non-integrable dynamical systems, which again lead to a form of chaos.

What is the basic idea of non-integrability in Poincaré's sense? Poincaré considered dynamical systems. They have kinetic energy and potential energy. He then asks the question, "Is there some clever transformation that would eliminate the interaction described by the potential energy so that the system would act as a set of independent particles?" In this case, the integration is very simple. He showed that, in general, this is impossible, and fortunately so; had the answer been in the affirmative, there would have been no possibility of coherence, of organization, of life. Interactions are, in general, irreducible. You cannot eliminate them. And Poincaré showed us why. Interactions are irreducible because of resonance between the various degrees of freedom.

I will not present the mathematics behind this, but let me make a vague analogy between this problem and playing the piano. When you play the piano, you play a fundamental tone, but you cannot avoid other tones and harmonics from sounding at the same time. The same sort of thing happens in dynamics. The non-integrability of systems such as Poincaré's, comes about as a consequence of resonances that couple events leading to dynamics, which results in a complex evolution of events because individual events cannot be separated. Instead, we must consider ensembles of events connected by resonance. The result is that we obtain, as in deterministic chaos, representations at the probabilistic level, which are irreducible. In other words, we obtain a formulation of laws of nature that includes Poincaré's non-integratibility, which can no longer be expressed in terms of trajectories or wave functions. In a sense, this comes about from the fact that the events are coupled, and this coupling leads to diffusive behaviour. Diffusion is described by a second order differential equation in space. This second order differential equation arises precisely through the coupling of the events through resonances. This is a very important result because it shows that, for chaotic systems in the sense of Poincaré, there is no determinism, since the basic equation now describes a diffusive process. If I start with a given point, I won't know where that point will go. Or starting with a given wave function, I won't know how that wave function will develop. Trajectories or wave functions may be destroyed by resonances. The microscopic description is then close to that of molecular chaos as associated to brownian motion. The basic dynamic description has to be expressed in terms of probability distributions, while trajectories, wave functions or fields, the traditional objects of physics, become approximations valid when the diffusive motion is negligible.

Where do these kinds of effects appear? I expect that in many cases these effects would be negligible. After all, we have verified quantum mechanics and classical mechanics in millions of situations. But we have also verified the predictions of kinetic theory — for example, the calculation of thermal conductivity from intermolecular forces using Boltzmann's equation — in millions of instances. Therefore, there must be situations where one type of theory is applicable, and situations where the other type of

theory applies. Briefly, the new type of theory involving resonances, dissipation, and indeterminism is valid when we have
persistent interactions. Persistent interactions appear, for example,
in liquids or in cosmology. They don't appear in the usual scattering experiment in which I prepare a wave packet, I shoot it at
an obstacle, and I look for times much longer than the duration
of the process. In contrast, the collisions between molecules in a
room go on forever. The interactions are persistent. In cosmology, likewise, we deal with persistent interactions. In all those
cases, the diffusive terms become essential exactly as would be
expected, because then we are dealing with thermodynamic systems. It is for these types of systems that we obtain the new
results. These results have already been verified in many computer experiments.

I believe that the opposition between the two views of time
and of nature, the static view and the evolving view, can now be
overcome. It can be overcome precisely by including instability in
the basic laws. After all, the evolutionary patterns of our universe
seem to be fundamental features of nature. In the *Scientific American*
issue mentioned above, you see that evolutionary patterns exist at
all levels in the universe. In fact, these evolutionary patterns have
been, in some sense, imposed on us by our experimental findings.
The existence of these patterns was not always accepted, much
like the bones of the Neanderthals which, when first discovered,
were regarded to be those of monsters, not the ancestors of human
beings. Therefore, the whole idea of time is, in a sense, imposed
upon us by our experimental discoveries, rather than originating *a
priori*. Today, theoretical physics has become an exception, an
island in which the laws of nature are still assumed to be time
reversible. This seems to me incongruous in the time irreversible
universe we observe. This new approach to physics and to time,
based on probabilities, also solves other problems like the quantum
paradox, associated with the collapse of the wave function, for
which there are many proposals. Some, like the "many worlds"
proposal and the role of consciousness, are quite fantastic. All of
them are purely verbal and not predictive of any new effects.

All this leads me to conclude that we are slowly overcoming what might be called the Cartesian dualism, in which, on one side, one has nature as an automaton and, on the other, the human observer outside nature. Einstein was very conscious of this problem, but he went too far when he postulated that the solution is to assume that human beings are also automatons, even if they don't know it. I remember reading with amusement a letter he wrote to Tagore in which he asked what the moon would answer if you asked it why it moves, and he said, "Well, the moon would probably answer that it moves because it likes to take a walk in the fresh air," or something along those lines. We smile when we hear this because we know that the moon moves because it satisfies Newton's laws. We should also smile when human beings are so pretentious as to believe that they do things because they have freedom of action; we know that the basic laws are deterministic and there is no reason to believe that determinism would stop when it reaches the human mind. Now, that is an extreme position. It amounts to assuming that everything is determined and, therefore, that even this lecture was pre-determined at the moment of the Big Bang some fifteen billion years ago. This seems to me unlikely. Chaos and instability lead to a different view. To some extent, they play for physics the role that natural selection plays in biology. Natural selection is a necessary condition for evolution, but it is not a sufficient condition; as Gould states in the *Scientific American* special issue, some species of bacteria, for example, have not evolved in three-and-a-half billion years. I am not a biologist, but I assume that Gould is right and there are some aspects of life that are evolving and some that are not, depending on the circumstances. Similarly, we see in the world around us that some aspects of matter have not evolved since the beginning of the universe. Everybody has heard about the black body background radiation that still surrounds us in the same state it was in nearly fifteen billion years ago. This black body radiation, by the way, contains most of the entropy in the universe, in the sense that there are a billion photons of the black body radiation for every single particle of matter. On the other hand, there are atoms and molecules that have evolved forming the basic building blocks of life.

I believe that the change from a deterministic point of view to one that recognizes the central role of probability and irreversibility is associated with a more optimistic view of nature and of the role of human beings. I have already quoted Einstein several times. At one point, he asks the intriguing question, "Who should do science?" His answer was "people who don't like to live in crowded environments, people who like to go to the high mountains to enjoy the fresh air, to be in harmony with nature." For Einstein, who is the greatest representative of classical science as the means for understanding nature, science was the way of transcending the tragedy of time. Einstein was living at a difficult historical moment, marked by wars and anti-Semitism. For him, science was a way of escaping the misfortunes of history. Is this still the role of science? Isn't the role of science today more about cleaning the polluted cities than escaping to the mountains?

What, then, is the role of science today? Let me finish with a very utopian, and also a very personal remark. I have always been interested in neolithic civilizations. As neolithic civilizations evolved into the historical civilizations, you find the appearance not only of great art, but also of division of labour and an increase in violence and inequality. This is apparent in the nature of tombs. In neolithic times, the tombs were the same for everybody. Contrast this uniformity with the pyramids of the pharaohs or the burial chambers of the emperors of China in historical times. In a sense, civilization was always marked by a double aspect: creating values, which are beneficial, but which seem to have been made possible only through the establishment of a system of systematic violence. This problem has still not been overcome. It is my hope, and it will not depend on science alone, that thanks to science, thanks to improved communications, we can build a world which will present less inequality, less inherent violence, while preserving the benefits of civilization.

GEORGE PORTER

Nobel Prize in Chemistry, 1967

*F*lash *photolysis is a method that induces a chemical reaction by shining a brief pulse of intense light through reactant molecules. A second flash illuminates the reaction zone, allowing researchers to observe and measure the reaction with a spectrometer as it is taking place. Short-lived intermediates — the chemical compounds formed by one reaction which then take part in another reaction — can be detected and give clues about the mechanism of the reaction taking place. George Porter, along with Manfred Eigen and Ronald Norrish, were awarded the Nobel Prize in chemistry in 1967 for their pioneering approach to the study of the pathways of fast chemical reactions.*

In the 1940s the light pulses used in flash photolysis were about 1/1,000 seconds in duration. Today, thanks to Porter and others, it is possible to peek into the lives of atoms and molecules on time scales faster than trillionths of a second — a ten-billion-fold improvement.

Porter's research over the years has become more interdisciplinary, melding his interest in flash photolysis chemical research with a wider interest of science. He has recently studied such processes as photosynthesis — the creation of sugar from carbon dioxide, water, and sunlight by green plants — using flash photolysis. The speed of the current lasers allows him to track the flow of energy through the chloroplasts (the centre of photosynthesis) of individual cells.

A native of Yorkshire, England, and a graduate of Leeds University, Porter joined Cambridge University in 1945 after several years in the Royal Navy volunteer reserve. He worked with Norrish on flash photolysis until 1948. Porter became director of the Royal Institution of Great Britain in 1966, a position he held until 1987.

George Porter is a Fellow of the Royal Society, of which he was president from 1985 to 1990. He was knighted in 1972, and made Lord Porter of Luddenham in 1990. He is currently professor and chair of the Centre for Photomolecular Sciences at Imperial College, London.

George Porter

CHEMISTRY
UNDER THE SUN

$\mathcal{F}$rom the day God said "Let there be light," photochemistry has been the power behind evolution. At first glance, evolution and the seemingly spontaneous creation of order out of chaos defies not only common sense but also the second law of thermodynamics. This law says that things mix but never unmix; burn but never unburn; wood disappears as smoke into the air, but we would be astounded if the opposite happened and a log of wood suddenly fell out of the sky. This same law also says that in any closed system — a system isolated from the rest of the universe and left to itself — the entropy, the disorder, and the chaos will increase.

Here is the key to the paradox. Fortunately, we and the Earth are not left to ourselves. We have an abundant source of energy, order, and negative entropy flowing to us from the sun. Together, the sun and the Earth obey the second law. They are running down to ultimate disorder and to the heat death where everything has the same temperature and nothing more happens. In the meantime, we earthly creatures bask in the sun, the driving force of evolution and the mainstay of life.

The engines of biochemistry are driven by the same laws as the steam engine. The sun is the furnace and the surface of the Earth is the condenser. But the engines driven by the sun are more sophisticated than Thomas Newcomen or James Watt could ever have dreamed of. They are the engines of photosynthesis, tiny engines in each individual cell of the green plant which together form the greatest power on Earth. We live not merely in a chemical world, but in a photochemical world, and without that light of the first day, the rest could not have happened.

The Darwinian changes occurred slowly, unnoticed by the participants who had little to say about the form their descendants would take. They merely fought to survive and, if they survived, they had the privilege of handing on their genes. The situation has changed drastically in the last few years. One species, humankind, now so dominates the Earth that it is in its power to eliminate most other species, as recently demonstrated with the smallpox virus. Those species that survive do so only because human beings find them interesting or useful, and we are interfering with the evolution even of these species. But it is only a matter of time before far greater powers will be in our hands. We are no longer pawns in this game. We are not even the kings and the queens. We are the players.

One of the oldest games we have played has been agriculture, where we have manipulated nature to our advantage for more than five thousand years. From where we stand today, that game has hardly begun. Agriculture is the latest of the applied molecular sciences. It is an old science, but the introduction of molecular biology into it has come late. All the powers of the chemist and the biologist will be applied to transforming the plant world. And considering that the plant world gives us all our food, nearly all our fuels, and materials with which to build and furnish our homes and to clothe ourselves, the potential for development can hardly be exaggerated — especially when the time comes that we can no longer rely on cheap supplies of fossilized vegetation, such as oil, coal, and gas. The question is whether life can continue to survive, as it has in the past, on the sun's energy harvested for us by photosynthesis.

During photosynthesis — the conversion of carbon dioxide, water, and sunlight into sugar — the sun pumps up the energy of the carbon dioxide and water, creating oxygen, food, and fuels. These fuels may now be burned in oxygen at a temperature of about 2,000 degrees or, with the help of enzymes, they can be eaten as food, combined with oxygen at a temperature of about 37 degrees (which is better for the digestion), and can generate the energy needed to sustain life. This conversion of sunlight into fuel is powered by the green engines, the chloroplasts found in the leaf cells. The chloroplasts contain a series of double membranes made of fat, called bilayer lipid membranes. They form the scaffolding for whatever else is contained in the chloroplasts, such as proteins and pigments. In the membranes are the cytochrome, the proton pump, and two green bodies known as photosystem 1 and photosystem 2, which pump electrons from one side of the membrane to the other. The overall process in which water is split and carbon dioxide reduced to make oxygen and sugars is quite complex. Altogether four electrons are required for every molecule of oxygen produced. These, in turn, require the absorption of eight photons.

The most important part of this vast photochemical system is photosystem 2, because it is the body in which water is split to give oxygen. This is really the heart of photosynthesis.

Two processes take place in a photosystem of this kind. The first is harvesting light energy through an antenna, and the second is the electron transfer in the reaction centre. The photons, or the energy absorbed in the chlorophyll or pigment molecules, hop from one molecule to another by a random walk mechanism. These molecules are very close together, their centres only about ten angstroms (1 ten-millionth of a centimetre) apart. The random walk has to be very, very fast, because otherwise the molecules will fluoresce and lose all their energy by re-emitting it as light.

If the energy is trapped by a pigment molecule before the energy is lost, that will drive an electron from a donor molecule to an acceptor molecule on the opposite side of the membrane, giving oxidation on one side and reduction on the other.

Let's have a look at what we know about photosystem 2. The structure of a few of these reaction centres has been determined in very great detail, but they are those of photosynthetic bacteria. The structure of the photosynthetic centres in the green plants is only just beginning to be solved. Photosystem 2 has been photographed recently by electron microscopy with image enhancement. It is a dimer — that is, two units together. Werner Kuhlbrandt has obtained the structure of the light-harvesting part of photosystem 2. You can't crystallize these units except in two dimensions, but, by using electron diffraction in two dimensions, one gets the structure in some detail. The light-harvesting unit has thirty-six chlorophyll molecules in all, but it can be broken down to monomers that are held together by protein. Looking at the overall structure, one really begins to ask what nature is playing at here. The structure is very random, with no particular sense or order about it. Yet we know it has to have order. We know these chlorophyll are only about ten, eleven, or twelve angstroms apart, centre to centre, and we know that if they get closer than that, the light harvesting is quenched. And we don't know what nature had in mind in producing a complicated structure like this for a light-harvesting unit, with so many monomers fused together, eventually creating a unit of some two hundred or so chlorophyll molecules.

We know quite a lot about how energy can pass from one unit to another in a light-harvesting structure. The process is somewhat similar to that in coupled pendulums, which all physicists know about. If pendulums are coupled, then setting one pendulum swinging will eventually result in the energy being transferred to the other, and, after a little while, the energy goes back to the first one as long as there is still coupling. The two molecules of chlorophyll follow the same pattern. They are dipoles (molecules with a negatively charged end and a positively charged end), and it is dipole–dipole coupling that transfers the energy from one to the other.

Light harvesting is very interesting and quite essential, but let me pass quickly to the reaction centre. We don't know the structure of the reaction centre, but we think there is a close homology between the amino acid sequences of photosystem 2 and that of photosynthetic bacteria, and we know a lot about the photosynthetic bacteria. What happens there is that one of the chlorophylls, a rather special dimer, gets light transferred to it by the energy transfer that I have explained, and then transfers an electron through a molecular chain up to pheophytin (chlorophyll with the magnesium missing) and to a quinone. On the oxidizing side, the manganese atoms are oxidized. Photosystem 2 has four manganeses, and it would be quite reasonable to guess that, since you need to transfer four electrons to produce one oxygen molecule, it is probably one manganese per electron, as the oxidizing power is accumulated. However, that is not certain. It may be that two are used twice.

I want to discuss briefly the kinetics of this time sequence. First, I'll digress to outline flash photolysis. The rates at which the processes I've just mentioned take place are extremely rapid. The way one studies these very fast reactions in chemistry and biology is to use two flashes of light. The first flash initiates the change; the second flash photographs what happened. As you increase the time interval between the flashes, you get a movie of what's happening. As one gets to very short times, you can't synchronize two flashes, so you use just one flash from a laser and split it into two. One half excites the molecules to cause the change, and the other half is sent on a little journey around the laboratory in order to delay it. You can get different delays by varying the length of the journey. For every millimetre, you get a delay of three picoseconds. In chemistry and biology there is little of value in measurements faster than a femtosecond because of the uncertainty principle. This principle states that the uncertainty in the energy at a femtosecond is a large fraction of the chemical bond energy itself.

Flash photolysis began forty-five years ago with milliseconds, and progressed very quickly to microseconds. Picosecond pulses, that is 10^{-12} of a second, became available in the 1980s as a result of the invention of the laser in 1960. We have relied on laser physicists to keep producing faster lasers that would do what we want. Currently we are in the femtosecond region. When photosystem 2 is hit with a femtosecond pulse, the first processes that can be measured are very fast indeed. They occur in about one-tenth of a picosecond. There are many ways of visualizing this speed. If this page is one picosecond in length, then to get to one second, you'd have to extend it to go around the world one thousand times. This is a very short time indeed. By hitting the photosystem 2 with different wavelengths and probing different wavelengths, we see a transfer of energy from one-half of photosystem 2 to the other, which is almost its mirror image. There are six chlorophylls in one of these units, and they are in slightly different environments. Some absorb at 680 nanometres, and some at 670. The transfer of energy from one of those pools to the other occurs with a lifetime of a hundred femtoseconds. Now, if we go to longer times, we can see the electron transfer. This occurs in twenty-one picoseconds, which starts off the chemistry — the oxidation of the water — and, eventually, the reduction of the carbon dioxide.

That is the basis of what happens in photosystem 2, and much of this is very recent. We are only just beginning to learn about these rates. You might say "So what? What does it matter whether it is twenty-one picoseconds?" In fact, the purple bacteria rhodopseudomonus viridis undergoes the same sequence, but the twenty-one picosecond electron transfer occurs in three picoseconds. And everyone is very surprised about that because the amino acid sequences in the two systems are almost exactly the same. It turns out that near where that electron transfer takes place, the purple bacterium has an amino acid called tyrosine, whereas the higher plant has another amino acid, leucine. Now, a recently discovered mutant of the bacterium that has leucine instead of tyrosine at that position, and the lifetime now increases from three picoseconds to twenty-one. I mention that as a possible answer to the question, "So what's the use?" The use is that by learning more about the structure and the dynamics — the rates — of these photoprocesses, we are preparing the way for genetic modifications. In fact, a change the other way from twenty-one to three picoseconds will increase the efficiency of that step by a factor of seven.

What I've discussed is connected closely to the question "How long can we survive?" Above all, we need energy to survive. There are conflicting opinions about when the oil and gas will run out, but they usually range around fifty years, plus or minus ten or twenty. But even if it is twice as long as that, it is going to run out eventually. So, finding a replacement for oil and gas is something we need to begin working on fairly soon. It is going to be a long haul. The answer to our energy needs may come to us through genetic engineering of plants. Of course, there are many other reasons for doing genetic engineering of plants — the improvement of crops of all kinds, the efficiency of crops, and all the other products — but I am going to look only at power.

Let us ask the very ambitious question, "Can these green engines produce all the power for all the people on Earth? Is there enough land?" Well, how much power do we need? The world consumes 8 billion tons of oil each year, 1.8 kilowatts per person. The average solar power is easily calculated. In Toronto, it is 170 watts per square metre. The peak is about 1,000 watts per square metre, but averaging for day and night, winter and summer results in the lower number. That means that over the Earth's surface, it is about 5,000 kilowatts per person, which is about 2,500 times more than a person needs. So, there is plenty of energy. If all you want is to be warm, you can use low-grade heat and do so with 100 percent efficiency. But if you want to get real power and turn it into electricity and free energy, then the efficiency is nothing like 100 percent and we must ask what it is.

What I have called thermodynamics includes restrictions due to the fact that the sun is white light and contains all wavelengths. Moreover, thermodynamics applies to everything, including photosynthesis. It applies to photovoltaic cells, for example, and 27 percent efficiency is about the best you can do there. Most of these restrictions can be countered and removed partially, except the thermodynamic ones. You can't get around the second law.

Having taken the thermodynamic restrictions of 27 percent into account there are still other sources of reduced efficiency. Eight photons are used in photosynthesis. But you need only 2.7 times the energy of a photon at 700 nanometres to bring about that reaction, which corresponds to 35 percent efficiency for that process. Then there is the problem of irradiation saturation. If you have a lot of light, the carbon dioxide concentration can't keep up with photosynthesis, and light, once again, is wasted. The reduction in efficiency due to saturation is harder to calculate, but it's about 33 percent. And there are other losses of efficiency such as light reflection and photorespiration, where the plant consumes itself or burns its own fuel. Altogether, that now comes to about 1 percent efficiency, which is approximately what is found in the field. You can do a little better in the laboratory, but not much. Photovoltaic cells in practice are as much as 20 percent efficient.

If we could do something better with photosynthesis, how much land would we need? There are approximately 4.4 billion hectares of cultivatable land in the world. At 1 percent efficiency of the conversion of solar power into usable power such as transportable fuels, we would need to use 500 million hectares to satisfy the world's fuel needs. That is 11 percent of the total cultivatable land. The power produced would amount to approximately 20 kilowatts per hectare. If it were possible to increase this efficiency to 5 percent, the land requirement would drop to 2.2 percent of the cultivatable land, which is an acceptable fraction of our cultivatable land to be used for fuel production. This is the goal and this is the hope. If we know more about photosynthesis, can we not improve this process? At present, some plants in the laboratory go up to 4 percent efficiency, but not throughout their whole life cycle. This is the challenge. To meet that challenge we have to begin by knowing more about the structure of the green engines and how they work. It may take a little time. Eventually, I can imagine, if all goes well, our future energy supply, when the fossil fuels run out, will all come from nuclear fusion — either a nuclear fusion reactor, which is yet to be made commercially, or that rather nice fusion reactor ninety-three million miles away, the sun.